8/08

Helling

Job Placement Strategies for Paralegals

WITHDRAWN

D1225546

WEST LEGAL STUDIES

Options.
Over 300 products in every area of the law: textbooks, CD-ROMs, reference books, test banks, online companions, and more – helping you succeed in the classroom and on the job.

Support.
We offer unparalleled, practical support: robust instructor and student supplements to ensure the best learning experience, custom publishing to meet your unique needs, and other benefits such as West's Student Achievement Award. And our sales representatives are always ready to provide you with dependable service.

Feedback.
As always, we want to hear from you! Your feedback is our best resource for improving the quality of our products. Contact your sales representative or write us at the address below if you have any comments about our materials or if you have a product proposal.

Accounting and Financials for the Law Office • Administrative Law • Alternative Dispute Resolution Bankruptcy • Business Organizations/Corporations • Careers and Employment • Civil Litigation and Procedure • CLA Exam Preparation • Computer Applications in the Law Office • Contract Law Court Reporting • Criminal Law and Procedure • Document Preparation • Elder Law • Employment Law • Environmental Law • Ethics • Evidence Law • Family Law • Intellectual Property • Interviewing and Investigation • Introduction to Law • Introduction to Paralegalism • Law Office Management Law Office Procedures • Legal Nurse Consulting • Legal Research, Writing, and Analysis • Legal Terminology • Paralegal Internship • Product Liability • Real Estate Law • Reference Materials Social Security • Sports Law • Torts and Personal Injury Law • Wills, Trusts, and Estate Administration

---

West Legal Studies
5 Maxwell Drive
Clifton Park, New York 12065-2919

For additional information, find us online at:
www.westlegalstudies.com

Job Placement Strategies for Paralegals

MARGARET E. PICKARD, J.D.

THOMSON

DELMAR LEARNING   Australia   Canada   Mexico   Singapore   Spain   United Kingdom   United States

WEST LEGAL STUDIES

Job Placement Strategies for Paralegals
by Margaret E. Pickard, J.D.

Vice President, Career Education Strategic Business Unit:
Dawn Gerrain

Director of Learning Solutions:
John Fedor

Managing Editor:
Robert Serenka

Acquisitions Editor:
Shelley Esposito

Editorial Assistant:
Melissa Zaza

Director of Content and Media Production:
Wendy A. Troeger

Content Project Manager:
Steven Couse

Art Director:
Joy Kocsis

Technology Project Manager:
Sandy Charette

Director of Marketing:
Wendy Mapstone

Channel Manager:
Gerard McAvey

Cover Images:
©istockphoto Inc.

Cover Design:
Suzanne Albertson

COPYRIGHT © 2008 Thomson Delmar Learning, a part of the Thomson Corporation. Thomson, the Star Logo, and Delmar Learning are trademarks used herein under license.

Printed in United States
1 2 3 4 5 XXX 10 09 08 07

For more information contact Delmar Learning,
5 Maxwell Drive, P.O. Box 8007, Clifton Park, New York 12065.

Or find us on the World Wide Web at http://www.westlegalstudies.com

ALL RIGHTS RESERVED. No part of this work covered by the copyright hereon may be reproduced or used in any form or by any means—graphic, electronic, or mechanical, including photocopying, recording, taping, Web distribution or information storage and retrieval systems—without written permission of the publisher.

For permission to use material from this text or product, submit a request online at http://www.thomsonrights.com

Library of Congress Cataloging-in-Publication Data:
Pickard, Margaret E.
  Job placement strategies for paralegals / Margaret E. Pickard.
    p. cm. — (West Legal Studies)
Includes index.
ISBN-13: 978-1-4180-4008-6
ISBN-10: 1-4180-4008-8
1. Legal assistants—Vocational guidance—United States. I. Title.
  KF320.L4P53 2007
  340.023'73—dc22
                          2007027031

NOTICE TO THE READER

Publisher does not warrant or guarantee any of the products described herein or perform any independent analysis in connection with any of the product information contained herein. Publisher does not assume, and expressly disclaims, any obligation to obtain and include information other than that provided to it by the manufacturer.

The reader is expressly warned to consider and adopt all safety precautions that might be indicated by the activities herein and to avoid all potential hazards. By following the instructions contained herein, the reader willingly assumes all risks in connection with such instructions.

The Publisher makes no representation or warranties of any kind, including but not limited to, the warranties of fitness for particular purpose or merchantability, nor are any such representations implied with respect to the material set forth herein, and the publisher takes no responsibility with respect to such material. The Publisher shall not be liable for any special, consequential, or exemplary damages resulting, in whole or part, from the readers' use of, or reliance upon, this material.

To My Students

CONTENTS

CHAPTER 8:   JOB SEARCH TECHNIQUES: WHERE TO START / 119

CHAPTER 9:   GET WIRED: FINDING ON-LINE JOB OPPORTUNITIES / 129

CHAPTER 10: PREPARING FOR THE INTERVIEW: THE FINAL STAGE / 135

CHAPTER 11: THE INTERVIEW: THE FINAL STAGE / 141

PREFACE

Opportunities are never lost, they're just found by someone else.

—Unknown

The paralegal profession offers exciting and rewarding careers for tens of thousands of individuals each year. While many paralegals are employed in traditional law firm settings, others work for government agencies, private corporations, or non-profit organizations. Some paralegals provide legal secretarial services while others research and write complex trial briefs for their supervising attorney. Although the role of the paralegal varies, the profession is more clearly defined than it was 20 years ago. Today, paralegals are an integral part of the legal community and firms are hiring paralegals to perform work that was once viewed as the sole domain of attorneys. As a result, the paralegal profession has become one of the fastest growing professions in the United States. To meet this growing demand, universities and other educational programs are turning out quality paralegals to join the legal profession.

This book targets paralegal students and professionals who are seeking to find opportunities in the workforce. While there are many generic job search books on the market, few offer practical advice that is specific to the paralegal community. The purpose of this book is to target this sector and present strategies to help paralegals prepare for, find, and obtain careers in the legal community, as well as related professions.

Job Placement Strategies for Paralegals will help you to prepare a winning resume that will highlight your strengths and catch the eye of prospective employers. In addition, you will learn how to write an effective cover letter, what I call your own personal "30-second Super Bowl Commercial." Once you have your resume and cover letter in your portfolio, you are ready to begin searching for your opportunities. Start networking with other legal professionals, contact employers listed on school job boards, search the internet, and explore all of your possibilities. Remember not to get discouraged in this process. When you do get your first interview, you need to make sure that you are prepared and professional. Interviewing techniques and questions are listed to help you get ready for an interview. Remember that an interview is a two-way street and while the employer wants to know if you are right for the job, you need to find out if the position fits your personal and professional needs.

Some paralegals dream of working for themselves and offering freelance services to the legal community. If this is an option you want to pursue, there are a several issues to consider, including ethical limitations and liability. This book offers a balanced viewpoint for consideration.

As you embark on your search for the ideal paralegal position, remember to keep your personal and professional goals in perspective. Many legal professionals commit their entire lives to their law firms and their clients, at the expense of their own personal lives. Throughout your career, try to maintain a balance that allows you to have personal satisfaction, professional commitment, and, perhaps most importantly, offers you an opportunity to contribute to your community.

ACKNOWLEDGMENTS

I am grateful for the contributions of the many individuals who helped me to develop this text. First, I would like to acknowledge Dan Barber and Alyssa Navallo, two nationally acclaimed paralegal educators who asked me to prepare job strategy materials and incorporate them into their paralegal programs offered throughout the country. They have significantly influenced my career as an educator, and I am grateful for their support and encouragement.

I am thankful to the many people who contributed directly and indirectly to this project. To my many students who provided their resumes and cover letters for inclusion in this work, thank you for allowing me to critique your documents publicly. Although your names and other identifying information have been changed, please know how grateful I am for your support and contributions. For all of those who edited my work, particularly Dean Flint and Cathy Kipp, two of my favorite people, thank you for your time and effort and for helping me to complete revisions. To my editors at Thomson Delmar Learning, Shelley Esposito and Diane Colwyn, thank you for your patience and support. Oh, and, of course, I am very grateful to Jenn Blackhurst, who forced me up before sunrise to keep me on schedule.

I am most grateful for the love and support of my wonderful husband, Keith, and our children. Thank you for believing in me. Keith, thank you for reading and re-reading all of these chapters and for encouraging me in everything I do. Stetson, someday I hope to have a million dollars to give you, but no amount of money can substitute for the love of my family. Dean, you're awesome, and I love the times we spend reading together. Bailey, you're beautiful, and your hugs keep me going every day. To my little Kathleen, may you always know that your soccer games really are the most important thing and I always try to make the right choice. Lisa, Rian, and Hayden, I am so thankful that you are in my life, and I love the time we spend together.

This work would not have been completed without all of these contributions, and I am grateful to all of you who made this project possible.

CHAPTER 1

GETTING THE JOB YOU WANT

The paralegal profession is one of the fastest growing fields. What does it take to find the perfect position?

JOB-HUNTING BASICS

- RESUME
- COVER LETTER
- JOB SEARCH
- INTERVIEWING

Finding your ideal job requires time, hard work, and patience. This chapter provides skills and strategies that will make your search more productive. It will help you to prepare a professional resume and cover letter, in addition to suggesting specific job search techniques. Once you find a job opportunity, you can prepare for the employer's interview by reviewing the tips and techniques given here, including what questions you should ask the interviewer. Following the simple steps and strategies outlined in this book will help you to feel more confident during your job search.

① READY: Prepare Your Resume and Cover Letter

Plan a Professional Resume

Before you begin your job search, you should prepare a resume that highlights your education, your experience, and your professional skills. Although most people know that they need a resume, most do not know how to prepare one.

Chapter 3 offers practical advice on creating a professional resume. The resume writing worksheet contained in Chapter 4 will guide you step by step through preparing your own resume, providing a framework to identify what information you should include.

Chapter 5 offers resume samples: the good, the bad, and the mediocre. These are real resumes prepared by paralegal students. Critiques and practical advice are offered for improving the format and the content of each sample. Review these resumes to find a format that appeals to you. Once you have perfected your own resume, you will need to prepare a cover letter that introduces you to a prospective employer.

LAW OFFICE MANAGER

"THINK OF YOUR RESUME AS YOUR PERSONAL ADVERTISEMENT. IF YOU WANT TO BE VIEWED AS A PROFESSIONAL, YOUR RESUME MUST BE PROFESSIONAL."

The Importance of a Cover Letter

The cover letter that accompanies your resume should be tailored to the specific employment position you are applying for. It is the first sample of your writing ability that the hiring firm will see. On the basis of this initial impression, the employer will assess whether you are a candidate capable of producing a professional document for his or her law office.

Too many people view a cover letter as something meaningless that reads only "Enclosed please find my resume." Instead, a cover letter should be a sales pitch that expresses your interest in the position and highlights your abilities and qualifications for the job. Chapter 6 will help you prepare a dynamic letter to grab your reader's attention. Chapter 7 offers samples, with critiques, to help you to see what works and what does not. This is an employer's first impression of you; make it a good one.

⏸ SET: Finding Job Opportunities

Most jobs are filled by someone the employer already knows or has heard about through a referral. This means that networking is one of the most effective ways of finding a job. So get to know people—people in your class, your instructor, members of the local paralegal association, and local attorneys. Of course, thousands of paralegal positions are advertised each year through local newspapers, job placement services, and employment agencies. In addition, hundreds of law offices need paralegals but have not yet advertised the position, so cold calling remains a very effective technique for finding these openings. Chapter 8 offers practical advice on how to find and create job opportunities; Chapter 9 provides specific guidance for on-line job searches.

▶ GO: The Interview

PARALEGAL RECRUITER

"JOB INTERVIEWS ARE A TWO-WAY STREET, AND APPLICANTS SHOULD ASK QUESTIONS TO DETERMINE WHETHER THE JOB IS RIGHT FOR THEM."

Once you find that perfect job opportunity, you will need to prepare yourself for the interview. Chapter 10 provides advice on preparing for the interview, and Chapter 11 lists typical questions you might be asked, including zingers such as "What would you identify as your biggest weakness?"

Most new job seekers make the mistake of thinking that an interview is a one-way street, a chance for the employer to see whether you are qualified for the job. In fact, it is also an opportunity for you to determine whether this job is right for you. Most employers appreciate an applicant who asks questions about the job, so Chapter 11 provides questions that will help you determine whether a job opportunity is as good at it sounds.

Be prepared to close the deal when a job offer comes your way. Before you receive the offer, you should have an idea of your minimum requirements. Have you ever created a written list of criteria for your ideal job opportunity? Chapter 12 offers considerations for determining whether a job meets your personal and professional criteria. It also offers suggestions on how you can tactfully keep a job offer open while you consider your options. In addition, it provides advice on negotiating a job offer that does not meet your minimum salary requirements or other criteria.

Finally, Chapter 13 addresses ethical considerations for those of you who want to be your own boss and "hang your own shingle." Working for yourself can be a great way to achieve some control over your own schedule; however, several issues need to be considered before you take this giant leap. Most states restrict paralegals from providing legal services directly to the public without attorney supervision. Although some states allow paralegals to offer document production services to the public, these services are coming under increasing scrutiny and regulation by most state legislatures. Therefore, freelance paralegals generally work on a contract basis for attorneys in the legal community. Before you fly solo, it is a good idea to work for an attorney to familiarize yourself with legal procedure and document drafting while you have someone readily available to answer your questions. These considerations, and others, are discussed in Chapter 13.

With all of these tools in hand, get ready . . . set . . . and go find that perfect job.

◉ Points to Consider

1. *Create a Career Inventory.* Identify the four most important factors in your job search, using the personal and professional considerations listed below.

   a.

   b.

   c.

   d.

   - work environment
   - job responsibilities
   - client contact
   - work hours
   - billable hour requirements
   - potential for advancement
   - salary offer
   - office staff
   - benefits package (health care, retirement, etc.)
   - personal economics (personal expenses, day-care costs, etc.)
   - location
   - travel time
   - transport costs
   - employment stability

2. *Create a Job Search Timeline.* Determine a realistic timeline to complete the following:

   a. prepare resume   *complete by:* _____

   b. draft cover letter   *complete by:* _____

   c. determine initial contacts   *complete by:* _____

◉ Job Search Tips

1. ***Research.*** Research job opportunities to determine employers' hiring criteria. Locate and review the following resources and strategies:
   - school postings
   - newspaper listings
   - paralegal/bar association postings
   - government listings
   - employment services
   - Internet searches
   - cold calling
   - networking
2. ***Network.*** Contact your local paralegal or bar association to make initial contacts in the legal community.

CHAPTER 2

THE ROLE OF A PARALEGAL IN THE LEGAL PROFESSION

"A great paralegal is the key to the success of a good lawyer."

—San Francisco litigator

DEFINING A PARALEGAL'S ROLE

A PARALEGAL IS A PERSON QUALIFIED BY EDUCATION, TRAINING OR WORK EXPERIENCE WHO IS EMPLOYED OR RETAINED BY A LAWYER, LAW OFFICE, CORPORATION, GOVERNMENTAL AGENCY OR OTHER ENTITY AND WHO PERFORMS SPECIFICALLY DELEGATED SUBSTANTIVE LEGAL WORK FOR WHICH A LAWYER IS RESPONSIBLE.[i]

ABA STANDING COMMITTEE ON PARALEGALS

PARALEGALS CAN BE A KEY ELEMENT IN FOSTERING COST EFFICIENCY OF A LEGAL TEAM.

Paralegals are integral to almost every law practice. The title "paralegal" was widely adopted after the American Bar Association (ABA) endorsed the use of paralegals in 1967. With the rapid growth of the legal industry during the 1970s, attorneys began to recognize the important role paraprofessional legal assistants could play in maximizing the productivity of a law practice. As this increased productivity translated into revenue, all segments of the legal community embraced the use of paralegals. Today, more than 225,000 paralegals are employed in the United States.[ii]

ⓘ READY: The Role of a Paralegal

Paralegals are often referred to as "legal assistants." Although the terms are considered interchangeable, much like "attorney" and "lawyer," most legal paraprofessionals prefer the term "paralegal." However, some states, such as California, require specific training before an individual can use the title "paralegal." For simplicity, the term "paralegal" will be used throughout this book.

Paralegals perform a variety of services; however, they cannot offer legal advice, represent a client in court, or set client fees. The ABA defines a paralegal as a person

> qualified by education, training or work experience who is employed or retained by a lawyer, law office, corporation, governmental agency or other entity and who performs specifically delegated substantive legal work for which a lawyer is responsible.[iii]

Paralegals can perform most tasks in a law office, provided an attorney supervises the work.[iv] However, typical paralegal duties include conducting client interviews, reviewing client files, organizing client documents, researching legal issues, preparing notices, drafting pleadings and discovery, scheduling, and summarizing depositions.

Although the paralegal profession is not specifically regulated, all 50 states prohibit the practice of law without a license. To safeguard against participating in unauthorized activities, paralegals should avoid working directly with clients without the supervision of an attorney. Paralegals can be prosecuted if they act in a representative capacity, and the most common pitfall is preparing legal documents directly for clients without review by an attorney. Such activities can and should be avoided.

⑪ SET: Licensing and Certification

Paralegals are not licensed as professionals. However, several national associations offer certification for paralegals. Certification requires that a paralegal demonstrate professional competence by meeting qualifying criteria and passing an examination administered by the association.

The ABA does not currently offer paralegal certification. The National Association of Legal Assistants (NALA) awards the designation "certified legal assistant" (CLA) or "certified paralegal" (CP); the requirements for certification can be found at the association's Web site (http://nala.org). The National Federation of Paralegal Associations (NFPA; http://www.paralegals.org) awards the designation "registered paralegal" (RP) to those who meet the appropriate criteria, including passing the Paralegal Advanced Competency Exam (PACE). These are the most common certifications for paralegals; however, other associations, such as the American Alliance of Paralegals (AACP; http://www.aapipara.org), also offer certification exams.

Certification indicates that candidates have met specified competency requirements and often have additional legal experience. Employers are generally willing to compensate applicants for this additional qualification and training. However, if you are not a certified paralegal, do not get discouraged; only a small percentage of all paralegals are certified, and most employers do not expect or require applicants to be certified.

▶ GO: Job Opportunities

The U.S. Department of Labor reports that 7 out of 10 paralegals work for private law firms; the others work for corporate legal departments and governmental agencies.[v] An increasing number of paralegals are also hanging up their own shingles and working as independent contractors, hiring their services out to attorneys.

It is projected that employment opportunities for paralegals and legal assistants will grow at a faster rate than the average for all occupations through 2014.[vi] Although it is anticipated that private law firms will continue to be the largest employer of paralegals, corporations, insurance companies, real estate firms, community-based legal services, and governmental agencies[vii] will also provide a growing number of jobs for paralegals.

Earnings

The earnings for paralegals and legal assistants vary significantly according to experience, area of practice, geographical location, and law firm economics. However, the reported median annual salary for paralegals in the United States is $40,000.[viii] To determine the earnings for your area, contact your state bar or local paralegal association. The Bureau of Labor Statistics also provides an annual overview of paralegal earnings available at http://www.bls.gov/oco/ocos114.htm.

The NFPA and the International Paralegal Management Association (IPMA) both publish a detailed annual survey of legal assistant compensation and management practices. The NFPA's annual Compensation and Benefits Study Report is available through its Web site (http://www.paralegals.org). The IPMA offers its guidebook, entitled *Annual Compensation Survey for Paralegals/Legal Assistants and Managers,* in association with Altman Weil Publications (available through http://www.paralegalmanagment.org). Several professional publications, including *Legal Assistant Today,* also offer salary surveys for paralegals.

Salary Expectations

Many people enter the legal profession with the mistaken impression that they will share in a law firm's multi-million-dollar settlements and court victories. The reality is very different. Attorneys are not permitted to split legal fees with paralegals, and paralegal compensation may not be contingent on the outcome of a particular case.[ix] However, paralegals can be paid discretionary bonuses on the basis of the overall success of a law practice.[x]

The practice of law provides great opportunities for those in the paralegal profession. However, if you are new to the profession, this will be reflected in your initial compensation package. Firms recognize that they will use time and resources to train a new paralegal in document preparation, legal research, discovery practices, and other relevant areas. Paralegals who have been in the profession for a number of years do not require extensive training and are generally more efficient at performing familiar tasks; their salaries reflect these cost savings to the firm.

Be realistic in your salary expectations as you look for a paralegal position. Sometimes, working for an initially low salary to gain experience will increase your future marketability and earning potential. Consider all factors when reviewing job opportunities.

Billable Hours Requirements

Many law firms have minimum billing requirements for paralegals, typically 20–30 billable hours per week. A billable hour is one spent in substantive legal work that can be billed directly to the client. However, clerical/secretarial tasks are considered part of office overhead costs and cannot be charged separately to a client. A general test of profitability applied in a law office setting is the "rule of three." That is, paralegals should generate revenue equivalent to three times their salary.

Say you go into the office at 8:00 a.m. and you review the mail and speak with your attorney about the day's schedule. At 9:00 a.m., you begin working on a lease for a client named Jim Smith. You work on the file until 12:00 p.m., when you go to lunch. When you return from lunch at 1:00 p.m., you do legal research for a client named Dean Flint. You continue that research until 5:00 p.m., but in the middle of the afternoon you receive a call from Jenna Brady, another of the firm's clients. You speak with Ms. Brady for 25 minutes about some discovery documents she is answering on her case. Before you leave the office at 6:30 p.m., you speak with your attorney for 15 minutes about an issue on the Mondave case. How do you bill all this? Assuming your firm bills on the basis of 15-minute increments, your daily timesheet should look similar to this:

Smith	3.0	Prepare Lease Agreement
Flint	3.5	Research Liability
Brady	0.5	Phone Call re: Discovery
Mondave	0.25	Conference with AG on Trial Preparation

Notice that you cannot bill for the time you spend on general office matters. Thus, in a 9.5-hour workday, you billed only 7.25 hours. Keep this in mind as you discuss billable hour requirements with a firm.

Now that you have an idea of just what you are getting into, get set to find that perfect job.

◉ Points to Consider

1. *Identify Professional Goals.* Identify, in writing, your professional career goals (e.g., document preparation, management responsibilities, participation in trial preparation).
    a. one-year goal:
    b. five-year goal:
    c. ten-year goal:
2. *Identify Personal Goals.* Identify, in writing, your personal goals.
    a. salary requirements:
    b. billable hour expectations:
    c. vacation and sick leave:

◉ Job Search Tips

1. *Research the Paralegal Profession.* See the U.S. Department of Labor, Bureau of Labor Statistics, *Occupational Outlook Handbook, 2006–2007 Edition,* "Paralegals and Legal Assistants" (http://www.bls.gov/oco/ocos114.htm) for an overview of job placement, salary, and demographics.
2. *Review Paralegal Web sites.* Find out more about the paralegal profession by visiting the following Web sites:
    a. ABA Standing Committee on Paralegals
        http://www.abanet.org/legalservices/paralegals

b. National Association of Legal Assistants, Inc.
http://www.nala.org

c. National Federation of Paralegal Associations
http://www.paralegals.org

● References

[i] American Bar Association (ABA) House of Delegates, 1997 (http://www.abanet.org/legalservices/paralegals/def98.html).

[ii] U.S. Department of Labor, Bureau of Labor Statistics, *Occupational Outlook Handbook, 2006–2007 Edition,* "Paralegals and Legal Assistants" (http:/www.bls.gov/oco/ocos114.htm).

[iii] ABA House of Delegates, 1997.

[iv] See ABA Model Guidelines for the Utilization of Paralegal Services (http://www.abanet.org).

[v] Bureau of Labor Statistics, *Occupational Outlook Handbook, 2006–2007 Edition.*

[vi] Ibid.

[vii] Within the federal government, the U.S. Department of Justice is the largest employer, followed by the Social Security Administration and the U.S. Department of the Treasury.

[viii] Bureau of Labor Statistics, *Occupational Outlook Handbook, 2006–2007 Edition.*

[ix] Guideline 9, ABA Model Guidelines for the Utilization of Paralegal Services.

[x] Rule 5.4(a)(4), ABA Model Rules of Professional Conduct (http://www.abanet.org/cpr/mrpc/rule_5_4.html).

CHAPTER 3

EFFECTIVE RESUME WRITING TIPS

The purpose of your resume is to win an interview.

YOUR RESUME

- CONTACT INFORMATION
- OBJECTIVE
- EDUCATIONAL BACKGROUND
- SKILLS
- WORK EXPERIENCE
- REFERENCE LISTING

Think of your resume as your personal billboard. It is not simply a listing of your employment history or your educational background; it is an advertisement of what you can offer a prospective employer. Research shows that on average employers grant one interview for every 50 to 100 resumes they receive. A prospective employer scans a resume in 10 to 20 seconds, so that is all the time you have to persuade the employer that you are the right candidate for the job. This means that the top half of the first page of your resume has to grab the employer's eye; otherwise, you will have lost his or her attention, and the interview.

Your resume is your personal advertisement, so tell the employer why you are more qualified for the job than the next candidate. Put yourself in the shoes of the employer: What would catch your attention if you were staring at 50 resumes and deciding which applicants to interview?

The Purpose of a Resume

A resume is your "calling card." If an employer is impressed by your resume, you will be called for an interview. A resume indicates whether you meet the employer's hiring criteria, offers a sample of your writing (and proofreading) ability, covers your educational background, summarizes your work experience, lists your contact information, and provides professional references (or indicates that they are available). The bottom line is that your resume should be an example of your ability to produce professional documents for the firm.

The question that haunts every applicant is "How long should my resume be?" Although there is no one answer for all candidates, in general it is best for paralegal applicants to limit their resume to one page. Paralegals with extensive experience or publications can and should provide longer resumes that highlight their experience and accomplishments, but, absent these exceptions, most applicants can condense their relevant experience to one page.

① READY: Hiring Criteria

A resume should indicate to potential employers that you meet their minimum hiring criteria, including educational background, experience, and other pertinent information. Therefore, as you prepare your resume, highlight the information from your background and experience that meets advertised requirements.

> ### Paralegal Position
> Large corporate firm seeks paralegal with five years' litigation experience in legal research and preparing and drafting pleadings, motions, and discovery. Fluent in Spanish. WPM 90.

Apply for jobs you are interested in even if you feel that you do not meet all of the listed requirements, such as work experience in the paralegal field. An employer who is looking for a paralegal with five years' litigation experience may also have an entry-level position for a new graduate, particularly if the firm advertises itself as a "large" firm. If you have two years' experience in another area of law, still apply for the advertised position. Employers are more likely to hire a candidate who is a "good fit" than an applicant who simply meets their stated hiring requirements.

Employers want to hire someone they like and would enjoy working with on a daily basis, so do not be discouraged if you find that you lack the requisite number of years working as a paralegal or extensive experience in a particular area of the law. Apply anyway. The worst that can happen is they say, "No thanks"; they may keep you in mind for a future position.

Writing Sample

Your resume is the firm's first impression of your writing ability. It should establish you as a professional with high standards and excellent writing and organizational abilities. Therefore, a resume should be clear, brief, well organized, well designed, and error free. It should have no spelling or grammatical errors.

Ask your instructor, a work associate, or a friend to review your resume for errors. They are more likely to catch mistakes than you are, particularly as you wrote the document. If English is your second language, ask a native speaker to review the content and grammar of your resume; it is not uncommon to make simple errors in verb tense or parallel construction.

Remember, your resume is your first writing sample. Obvious mistakes in a resume indicate that the writer is not a detail oriented, careful, and conscientious worker. Make the first impression a good one: PROOFREAD.

⏸ SET: Start Writing Your Resume Today

Too many people get bogged down trying to write the perfect resume. If you spend two weeks writing your resume, that is two weeks of interviews you will miss out on. It is better to write a quick draft of your resume to give you a jump start and then review it over the next few days to perfect it. Use the worksheet in Chapter 4 to put together the information you will need to include on your resume—then begin the layout of your resume.

Formatting Your Resume

A resume is your professional picture. It demonstrates not only who you are and where you have been but also where you want to be professionally. Observing a few basics in drafting your resume will help you compile the information that will highlight your potential.

Choosing the Format

Many formats are available for the presentation of your resume, including the chronological resume, the functional resume, and the hybrid resume. The chronological resume is hands-down the top choice for law firms, because it is the easiest to review. The chronological resume presents your education and work experience in reverse chronological order, with the most recent degree or job position listed first.

In contrast, the functional resume is often used by applicants who have been out of the job market for an extended period or who are older and do not want to highlight their age. This format emphasizes what work the applicant has done but not where or when the applicant performed the work. For example, a functional resume might list "Document Preparation" and "Legal Research Assignments" or otherwise provide a general listing of work performed in a previous career. Although the functional format does draw attention to an applicant's key strengths, while removing the chronological information, it has significant drawbacks. Employers often view a functional resume as an attempt to hide negative information in the applicant's background, and they may not review the resume.

Some applicants use a hybrid form of the chronological and functional resumes to highlight their accomplishments without omitting chronological information. The hybrid resume offers an introductory "Skills" section listing specific strengths, job functions, and skills. This section is followed by an "Experience" section similar to the chronological resume. This format is a good option if you find that you have large gaps in your employment that cannot otherwise be filled (e.g., with volunteer experience) or if you do not want to highlight that you are in your golden years. I find it interesting that many applicants do not want employers to know their age, particularly at a time when employers are becoming increasingly appreciative of the experience and work ethic of older employees. Do not assume that your age is a barrier to employment; you may find the opposite effect with many employers.

In deciding which of these formats to use, you should keep in mind that most law firms prefer the chronological format. If you need to modify the format to fit your specific circumstances, this can be done within the general layout.

Layout

The layout of your resume should be clean and easy to read. You should format your resume so that your reader can easily identify your qualifications, including educational background, work experience, and related information. This may require condensing years of work experience into a brief listing of positions held, possibly even omitting some of your work experience.

Sounds overwhelming? It does not have to be if you ask yourself this simple question: What education or experience do I have that is relevant to a career as a paralegal? This can be a laundry list of positions, but generally it includes work experience that demonstrates research/writing ability, management experience, interpersonal (people) skills, and job commitment. In listing and describing your work history, think about how your past experience relates to the duties required of a paralegal.

In preparing your resume, consider the following basics for formatting:

- use bullet headings rather than a narrative form
- use action words
- use white space effectively
- limit your resume to one page if possible—two if you cannot condense your education and experience into one page

Bullet Headings. Bullet headings rather than a paragraph of text will make your resume more readable. It is easier for a potential employer to scan the contents of a resume when bullet headings are used.

Remember, an employer spends only 10 to 20 seconds reviewing a resume, so make it easy for the reviewer to find the information that can help you land the job.

Narrative Form vs. Bullet Headings

Stan & Hope, *Paralegal, Los Angeles, California*

Prepared and drafted complaints, answers, requests for admissions, requests for production, interrogatories, and motions for dismissal, motions for summary judgment, and other legal documents. Responsible for client intake interviews, consulting with clients in document preparation, and updating clients regarding the status of their cases.

Stan & Hope, *Paralegal, Los Angeles, California*

- Drafted pleadings, motions, and discovery documents
- Conducted client interviews
- Client liaison

Action Words. Use action words when preparing your resume. Action verbs are preferable to the passive voice ("research was conducted") and generally more direct in terms of identifying your qualifications. Actions word include the following:

researched	conducted	presented	identified	analyzed
produced	created	assessed	initiated	briefed
prepared	coordinated	investigated	represented	developed
maintained	facilitated	negotiated	established	organized

White Space. White space is blank space. A resume that has adequate white space is easier to read because information is not crammed onto the page and the reader can skim the contents. White space should be evenly distributed over the entire page to give the appearance of balance.

The importance of white space is often overlooked by applicants who are attempting to include every last detail of their work history on a resume. A resume should be a "glimpse" of the applicant, providing an overview of the candidate's qualifications, sparking the interest of the employer, and generating an interview. So, remember, white space is an important aesthetic consideration.

Keep It Short. A paralegal resume should generally be limited to one page, unless you have extensive experience in the legal profession or a related field. Remember, an employer typically scans a resume in 10 to 20 seconds, so the most important portion of your resume is the top half of the first page. If you catch the employer's attention during this initial scan, you are more likely to have your entire resume reviewed.

If you feel that you cannot condense your educational background, your work experience, and your skills listing into one page, make sure that page two of your resume provides identifying information in case it is separated from page one.

Julia Wright
Page 2

Employ the basics of formatting to produce a professional resume that catches an employer's attention and invites an interview. Use bullet headings, action words, white space, and brevity if you want your resume to stand out from the crowd.

The Elements of Your Resume

Your resume should always contain these basic elements: contact information, objective, educational background, and work experience. Sometimes, you will also have a skills or reference listing.

Contact Information

Provide your full name, address, home phone, cellular phone, and e-mail address to allow the employer to contact you. This information should be prominently given at the top of your resume.

Gene Davis Jr.

4567 Sienna Heights Road   cell   555.243.7678
Summerlin, Nevada 89079   555.808.7965

GeneDavisJr@aol.com

The address that you list on your resume should be a permanent one, or at least one that you plan to be at during the interview process. If you do not have a permanent address, use the address of your parents or a friend. If you use an old address, it can take days or weeks to receive mail that has been forwarded. By the time you receive the mail, the employer may have already filled the position, assuming that you were not interested.

Make sure that you are available to answer calls from prospective employers. Because, realistically, you will miss a few calls, record a professional greeting that provides your full name (not your nickname), as well as a sample of your phone voice and your phone etiquette. Employers are not impressed when they reach an answering machine that greets them with "Hey babe . . . Thanks for calling Rob's Hangin' Place. Can't speak at you now, so leave a message and maybe I'll call back." This certainly would not win you an interview.

If you want to list two numbers, such as your cellular and a home number, list your preferred number first. Employers will most likely call the number listed first and, if they leave a message, may not try the second number. If you have young children at home who have questionable phone manners or may forget to take a message for you, it might be wise to list only a cell phone number. This should ensure that you answer the phone, you control the phone messaging system, and you receive all information about a job opportunity.

Make sure to check your messages frequently during your job search. Whether you return phone calls promptly will reflect your degree of professionalism. An applicant who does not return a phone call for several days may lose out on an opportunity to interview for the position.

Do not list your current work phone number on your resume unless you can comfortably discuss another job opportunity within earshot of your employer. Most applicants who are employed prefer that their current employer not know that they are looking for another position. Discovery would have a chilling effect on opportunities for advancement in your current firm if you do not find another job.

An e-mail address such as charliesbaby@aol.com is not professional. Create an e-mail address that is based on your name or your career. An e-mail address should locate you and allow an employer to reach you with a brief note; therefore, it is best to use your name, or a portion of it (e.g., sarahjones or sjones), or to choose a "legal" e-mail address (paralegalresearcher@cox.net). Many graduates use their name and the school that they attended (e.g., DeannaScottUNLV@cox.net).

It is not advisable to use your work e-mail address. Prospective employers will frown on an applicant who uses company time and

---

MANAGING PARTNER

"I RECENTLY ATTEMPTED TO CONTACT AN APPLICANT TO INVITE HER TO A SECOND INTERVIEW. HOWEVER, WHEN I REACHED HER ANSWERING MACHINE, I WAS SURPRISED BY HER GREETING, 'TOO BAD YOU MISSED ME . . . IT'S YOUR LOSS. LEAVE A MESSAGE AND MAYBE I'LL GET BACK TO YOU.' IT WAS REALLY TOO BAD FOR HER THAT SHE MISSED ME; I DIDN'T LEAVE A MESSAGE OR FOLLOW UP FOR A SECOND INTERVIEW. I DID NOT FEEL THAT SHE WOULD PROPERLY REPRESENT OUR FIRM'S STANDARDS."

AN E-MAIL ADDRESS SHOULD BE PROFESSIONAL. USE YOUR NAME OR YOUR INITIALS, OR INCLUDE THE UNIVERSITY YOU ATTENDED.

resources to answer personal e-mails. In addition, your current employer will not appreciate you using their resources to find another job.

Objective

An "Objective" section, which indicates the type of job you are seeking, is optional. Many applicants shy away from including one because it does not provide additional information about their qualifications. However, such sections can be important, particularly if your cover letter is separated from the resume. Some employers with large human resources departments (e.g., corporate offices, casinos) automatically discard resumes that do not clearly indicate the position sought. On the other hand, if you define your objective too narrowly (a paralegal position concentrating on estate planning), you may exclude yourself from other opportunities and other jobs.

Most statements of objective are boring and do not catch the eye of the reader. Consider highlighting some of your qualifications in the "Objective" section; this is a great way to present experience and skills. Be confident and tell the employer what skills you have to offer a law firm.

> ### Objective
> To obtain a paralegal position as a bilingual speaker with experience drafting pleadings, discovery, and motions who offers excellent computer skills, including proficiency in using Windows, Word, Excel, PowerPoint, Lotus, WESTLAW, and Lexis-Nexis.

Some employers consider the "Objective" section unnecessary if your cover letter indicates the type of job for which you are applying. Many resume writing experts suggest that the section be included only if the applicant lacks sufficient experience to show a logical career path. That is, if your work history does not indicate that you are looking for *another* paralegal position, an "Objective" section is useful.

If you do include an "Objective" section, make sure that it tells your reader why you are qualified for the position. Employers hate to read a fluff piece that provides little or no information about the applicant.

Educational Background

Your educational background is important when you have specialized training, such as your paralegal certificate. In such situations, it is best to list your education in reverse chronological order.

List your degrees and certificates as well as memberships and achievements during your training program. Do not be shy; brag, but be brief about it. In listing your education and training, include seminars, job training courses, continuing education courses, and other relevant experience. Provide details about the training you received if you need to "beef up" this section. This listing will also demonstrate your desire for continued education.

2007 Paralegal Studies Certificate,
University of California, Berkeley

- Coursework in legal terminology, legal writing, interviewing, field investigation, arbitration procedures, and legal research
- Legal document preparation, including pleadings, discovery, motions, and service of process
- Substantive emphasis on family law and business law

2000 Bachelor of Arts, Sociology,
University of California, Davis

- *Emphasis*, law and society
- *Minor*, Spanish

Skills

Many applicants include a "Skills" section between their educational background and work experience. If you are proficient in using particular computer programs (e.g., Word, Outlook, Excel, Access, Photoshop, PowerPoint), billing software (e.g., QuickBooks), or electronic legal research tools (e.g., Lexis-Nexis, WESTLAW) or you offer a unique or otherwise appealing skill (e.g., fluency in a foreign language), consider adding this information in a separate section. This will highlight the information and add credibility to your resume.

Work Experience

Are you one of those job seekers who do not think your work history has anything to do with working in the paralegal profession? Have you ever considered that a hairdresser has developed people skills, a massage therapist has learned listening skills, and a casino pit supervisor has managerial experience? Make a list of your work experience and then list the duties and skills that could relate to working as a paralegal (e.g., organizational skills, people skills, writing ability, management experience). It is amazing how most job skills are transferable into the legal profession.

This section can be labeled "Work Experience," "Work History," "Professional Experience," "Related Experience," "Experience," or "Other Experience." Do not use this section to list every job that you have ever held. Choose those jobs that are relevant to the position you are seeking as a paralegal and list them in reverse chronological order. If you have extensive work experience, you can list employers and positions without detailing job responsibilities; such a listing helps to condense information on your resume.

If you have gaps in your employment history, consider listing any volunteer work you were involved in during these periods. Volunteer work is very valuable and shows your ability to interact with the community (translation: your ability to bring in business for the firm).

Generally, it is best to list the month and year that you began and left each job (e.g., August 2003 to July 2004). However, if you have extensive gaps in your work history, consider listing only the years that you worked with a particular employer; this allows you to blur your employment history.

In writing about your work experience, use short sentences or even fragments (e.g., "Responsible for customer relations"). Do not use a narrative form, because a prospective employer will skim over your story. Instead, use bullets to set out your job duties/responsibilities.

Narrative Form vs. Bullet Headings

Supercuts, *Shift Manager*   April 2002 to June 2002

Having been a manager for this company in Nevada I was able to give support to the store manager and maintain business in her absence. I was responsible for managing and directing employees during my shift and troubleshooting any occurrences during such times. Several of my other job duties included record keeping, balancing the cash drawer, and maintaining morale of the shop. During this time I also demonstrated self-discipline and client loyalty while continuing to work in Las Vegas.

Supercuts, *Shift Manager*   April 2002 to June 2002

- Managed and directed employees
- Maintained record keeping of daily accounts

The narrative form is generally too wordy and will lose the reader's eye. Look at your resume for 30 seconds and ask yourself which top five points stand out. You will find that using bullets points draws the eye to the writer's key points.

Reference Listing

Giving the names of references is best reserved for the interview. In considering individuals who can provide a recommendation for you, do not list family members, personal friends, or others who have not worked with you in some capacity. References should be able to answers the questions asked by prospective employers, such as "Is Joe a good employee?"; "Is he a conscientious worker?"; "Is he prompt in completing his assignments?"; "Does he work well with others?" If your references are not listed on your resume, you should have a typed listing to provide to an employer during an interview.

Remember to check with your references *before* you provide their names and contact information to a prospective employer. Be sure to ask your references whether they will give you a positive recommendation. If they hesitate, you may want to reconsider listing them.

▶ GO: Start Writing Your Resume

A final point about preparing your resume is to be scrupulously honest. Do not inflate your qualifications (e.g., do not round a 3.78 GPA to a 3.8 GPA). Employers can and do check the information listed on your resume, and any discrepancies will leave you out of the running for a position with the firm.

A resume opens the door to a job opportunity; however, it is only the first step. A well-written resume may get you a job interview. Then you have to demonstrate to the employer during the interview that you are qualified for the job because you have the required skills, the professionalism to represent the firm, and a personality that fits in with the existing office personnel. So, before you begin writing, ask yourself: "If I were the employer hiring for this position, what would be important to me?" Answer that question as you begin drafting your own resume using a resume worksheet.

◉ Points to Consider

1. *Determine Your Job Objective.* Prepare a two-sentence written description of your job objective in the space provided below.

2. *References.* Contact three past supervisors or employers who can serve as employment references for you. Confirm that each contact will provide a positive reference for you as an employee.
   Reference #1:
   Name of supervisor/employer:
   Company:
   Street address:
   City, state   zip code:
   Phone contact:
   Reference #2:
   Name of supervisor/employer:
   Company:
   Street address:
   City, state   zip code:
   Phone contact:
   Reference #3:
   Name of supervisor/employer:
   Company:
   Street address:
   City, state   code:
   Phone contact:

◉ Job Search Tips

1. *Research Resume Builders.* If you are having trouble getting started, research on-line resume builders available at sites such as http://www.usajobs.opm.gov, http://www.monster.com, and http://www.resumebuilder.com.

2. *Consider the Professionalism of Your Contact Information.* Review your contact information to determine whether it is professional. Confirm that your answering machine/service provides an appropriate message for employers attempting to contact you. In addition, determine whether your e-mail address is professional; if not, consider creating a new address for your job search.

3. *Review Resume Samples.* Review the sample resumes in Chapter 5 to find a format that appeals to you. Copy relevant sections to use in your resume.

CHAPTER 4

GETTING STARTED BUILDING YOUR RESUME

A resume worksheet will help you identify the information you should include in your resume. Let's get started.

START WRITING

- COMPLETE THE WORKSHEET
- CHOOSE A RESUME TEMPLATE
- PREPARE A DRAFT
- PROOFREAD

This chapter includes a worksheet to help you prepare and organize the materials for your resume. Use it to draft the material that you will include in your resume.

ⓘ READY: Think About Your Qualifications

Each section of the resume worksheet briefly describes the material you should include under the heading and how it should be presented. For example, when you detail your educational background, it is customary to list it in reverse chronological order. Similarly, in addressing work experience, you may want to list relevant volunteer work, particularly if there are large gaps in your paid employment history. Review the instructions at the beginning of each section as you consider the information that you will include in your resume. Helpful hints and guidance are offered as you prepare each section.

ⓘ SET: Review Sample Resumes

You will find it helpful to review the sample resumes, with critical comments, contained in Chapter 5. This overview of good, bad, and mediocre resumes is intended to guide you in considering the format and content of your resume.

Once you have completed the worksheet, use a resume template to help you plug the information into a workable resume format. Many templates are available commercially. Figure 4.1 provides a sample template for your consideration.

FIGURE 4.1

Your Full Name

Street Address   Phone Contact

City, State   Zip Code

E-mail Contact

OBJECTIVE
State your job objective.

EDUCATION
Name of Educational Institution
Type of Degree, Year Earned
* *Bullet 1: Description of degree program*
* *Bullet 2: Substantive courses completed*
* *Bullet 3: Awards received*
(Repeat for all higher education degrees and relevant certifications.)

WORK EXPERIENCE
Employer Name, *Location*
Job Title, Employment Dates
* *Bullet 1: Description of job duties*
* *Bullet 2: Description of job duties*
* *Bullet 3: Particular employment accomplishments*
(List most recent job first. Repeat for additional jobs.)

SKILLS
* *Computer proficiency*
* *Other skills*

▶ GO: Your Resume Worksheet

Complete the following worksheet to determine what information you want to include on your resume.

Contact Information

Your contact information should provide an address where you check your mail regularly and where you will receive mail for as long as your resume is active. The phone number you list as a contact should be a number where you can easily be reached. In case you cannot answer when an employer calls, make sure that you have an answering service/machine with a professional message so that the employer can leave a message.

Name:

Address:

Cell phone:

Home phone:

E-mail address:

Job Objective

This section indicates the type of job you are seeking and offers you an opportunity to highlight one or two of your qualifications. Limit your objective to a few short sentences. Some employers consider this section unnecessary. Many experts recommend including this section only if you lack sufficient work experience to show a logical career path.

Education and Training

If you have post-secondary education or training (college degree, certificate, etc.), it should be listed after your objective. *List education in reverse chronological order (most recent certificate/degree first).* Provide the name of the institution (in bold type), the degree received (bold and italics), and the year you received it (if the degree is less than 15 years old) or expect to receive it (e.g., "Certificate expected spring 2008"). If your degree is in a field other than paralegal studies, you do not need to provide specific information for college degree coursework, other than your major and, if applicable, minor. If you have received awards or other recognition for courses or seminars, offer a listing.

Education and Training (e.g., paralegal degree or certificate)

Institution:

Degree or certificate:

Specific substantive courses completed:

Document preparation experience:

Awards, achievements, and extracurricular activities:

Other relevant information:

Education and Training (college/post-high school)
Institution:

Degree or certificate:

Specific courses/programs related to the job objective:

Awards, achievements, and extracurricular activities:

Other relevant information:

Armed Services Experience
Institution/training facility:

Rank:

Courses/programs related to the job objective:

Awards, achievements, extracurricular activities:

Related Professional and Educational Seminars

Local paralegal associations generally offer their members educational seminars at monthly or quarterly meetings. Perhaps you have attended a National Notary Association seminar or a Secretary of State training session.

Professional Organizations

Consider joining a local paralegal association or the paralegal division of your state bar association. The National Association of Legal Assistants and the National Paralegal Association offer excellent resources for paralegals.

Work Experience

Organize this section by listing the job positions you have held in reverse chronological order (that is, the most recent job first). Include volunteer work, particularly if you have gaps in your employment history. Provide the name of your employer (in bold type), the city (italics), the job title (bold and italics), and the start and end dates of your employment (month/year). Include a brief listing (complete sentences are not required) of your job duties. Even if you have not worked in the legal field, note relevant experience such as customer service, management experience, and writing skills. If you have worked for one employer for a long time but have held different job positions, list each position separately if you have room on your resume.

Most Recent Position

Name of employer:

Address (city and state):

Job title:

Employment dates (beginning and ending):

Brief description of relevant experience/responsibilities:

Additional Employment

Name of employer:

Address (city and state):

Job title:

Employment dates (beginning and ending):

Brief description of relevant experience/responsibilities:

Additional Employment

Name of employer:

Address (city and state):

Job title:

Employment dates (beginning and ending):

Brief description of relevant experience/responsibilities:

Additional Employment

Name of employer:

Address (city and state):

Job title:

Employment dates (beginning and ending):

Brief description of relevant experience/responsibilities:

Other Work-Related Experience

Volunteer Experience

The section is necessary only if you have large gaps in your employment history. However, if you have extensive volunteer experience, you may want to include this as a separate section to show your commitment to and involvement in the community. If your volunteer work is political or religious in nature, you may want to consider whether it is wise to include it. Job candidates often feel strongly about their political and/or religious convictions and want employers to be aware of this; such information can work for or against you.

Name of agency/company:

Address (city and state):

Volunteer dates (beginning and ending):

Volunteer position:

Brief description of relevant experience/responsibilities:

Hobbies/Interests

This section is optional. Consider including hobbies and interests if you need to fill some white space or you have a passion for a particular sport or hobby. A listing of hobbies or interests can break the ice and spark a conversation with an interviewer.

Reference Listing

References should not generally be listed on your resume; more commonly, they are provided to a prospective employer at the interview. In preparing this list, consider people who will provide a positive reference for you. Do not list family members, personal friends, or others who have not worked with you in some capacity. References should be able to answers questions from prospective employers such as "Is Joe a good employee?"; "Is he a conscientious worker?"; "Is he prompt in completing his assignments?"; "Does he work well with others?" *Remember to check with your references* before *you give their names and contact information to a prospective employer.*

Name of reference:

Position (vice president, supervisor, human resource manager, etc.):

Agency/company address (city and state):

Phone contact/e-mail contact:

Additional References

Name of reference:

Position (vice president, supervisor, human resource manager, etc.):

Agency/company address (city and state):

Phone contact/e-mail contact:

Resume Samples: Getting You Started

Most legal resumes follow a standard format, as illustrated in Figure 4.1. The samples in Chapter 5 show options for formatting a resume, and a resume template is also available in Appendix A. Choose the format that works best for you and insert the information from the worksheet into your chosen format.

◉ Points to Consider

1. *Ask for Input.* Sometimes it is hard to recall educational accomplishments, work history, and other relevant information to include in your resume. Contact family members and friends to ask them for a listing of your personal and professional highlights. Parents often will remember important information that you have omitted from your resume.

2. *Volunteer Experience.* Review the work history you have listed to determine whether major gaps appear in your employment timeline. If you have a gap of one year or more, consider listing volunteer/community service during this period.

◉ Job Search Tips

1. *Prepare to Complete Job Applications.* Maintain your interview worksheet; it can provide information that you may

need, and that may not be available on your resume, in the event an employer asks you to complete a job application at the time of an interview.

2. ***Research Job Opportunities.*** Begin identifying and listing job opportunities through your school's job board, newspaper advertisements, paralegal associations, on-line listings, and other postings. List three job opportunities that appeal to you:

Opportunity #1:
Employer:
Contact:
Hiring criteria:
Opportunity #2:
Employer:
Contact:
Hiring criteria:
Opportunity #3:
Employer:
Contact:
Hiring criteria:

CHAPTER 5

EVERYONE'S AN EXPERT
Good, Bad, and Mediocre Resumes

Everyone's an expert when it comes to helping you prepare and write your resume. Listen to the advice and adopt the ideas that work best for you.

RESUME BASICS

- KEEP IT SHORT
- HIGHLIGHT YOUR STRENGTHS
- BE PROFESSIONAL
- PROOFREAD

When you are preparing your resume, you will discover that everyone is willing to give you advice on how to do it: "A resume should be only one page, two if you have a lot of relevant experience"; "List your references"; "Never list references"; "List your education first"; "List your work experience first"; and on and on. Obviously, there is not just one way to write a resume; there are hundreds.

① READY: Review Sample Resumes

This chapter provides examples of paralegal resumes. Comments offer guidance on both the good and bad points in each. Find a style that works for you and prepare your own resume. The key points to remember in writing your resume are to keep it short, highlight your strengths, make it look professional, and proofread. Just one mistake in your resume can mean that it is taken from the "interview" pile and tossed on the "throw away" pile.

Creative Resume Ideas

Employers receive hundreds, sometimes thousands, of resumes every year. For this reason, applicants have come up with a variety of ways to make their resume stand out. The following ideas are definitely creative, but they would be considered very unusual in a law firm environment:

- a box of chocolates delivered to the managing partner, with a resume inside
- a bouquet of flowers with a resume attached as the "gift card"
- a singing telegram about an applicant—with the resume delivered, of course

- lunch sent from a local restaurant courtesy of an applicant, with the resume included (so that the prospective employer can at least send a thank-you note)
- a bouquet of helium balloons with a resume tied to the bottom

Are these really such crazy ideas? Some are, but they definitely would help an applicant to be remembered.

It would be too expensive to try this approach with every job, and, frankly, if your resume is good enough, these ideas are unnecessary. Do bear in mind that most law firms are fairly conservative, so if you choose to be creative, keep it within appropriate bounds. Law firms are not looking for creativity; they are looking for individuals who present a professional image.

⏸ SET: Your Resume Should Be Unique

Every resume will ultimately be unique, because every person has a different work history and educational background. So feel free to use any portion of the wording or formatting in the sample resumes that follow. Choose a layout that appeals to you and tailor the document to your qualifications.

Commentaries on the Sample Resumes

The commentaries on each sample resume note the strengths and weaknesses of the presentation, the material, or the format. These commentaries are intended to highlight some of the common pitfalls in resume writing (such as cramming too much information on to a page) and to point out good drafting ideas.

Remember, the purpose of a resume is to secure an interview not to provide a listing of your work history. You have only 10 to 20 seconds to catch the employer's attention; make the top half of your resume identify you as the ideal candidate.

▶ GO: Key Points to Remember

- a resume should be only one or two pages long
- list your strongest points on the top half of the first page
- prepare a professional resume
- provide plenty of white space
- proofread, proofread, proofread

FIGURE 5.1

Great layout but this resume needs more substance

Some employers might think this objective is too simplistic

Provide job title

What did she do in Human Resources?

The job descriptions should provide more detail

Capitalization is inconsistent throughout resume

The verb tense does not agree throughout

Use bold and italics to emphasize the program and university

Her bullets do not align; this is bad form

This is too much white space for the bottom of the document

5926 Cypress Court   415.555.4356
San Francisco, CA 94143   LaceyPatten@cox.net

Lacey M. Patten

Objective   To obtain a Paralegal Position with your organization.

Experience   2003 – 2004 Universal Fidelity Corporation   San Francisco, CA
                     Collections
                     • Administrative Assistant to regional manager.
                     • Supervisor of large balance collectors.
                     • Human Resources.

                     2000 – 2002 Fairfield Resorts   Reno, NV
                     Collections
                     • Responsible for over 500 accounts.
                     • Maintaining accounts up to Date.
                     • Implemented training course for new collectors.

                     1996 – 2000 Richy's Locker Mini Storage   Pahrump, NV
                     Property Manager
                     • Leasing Storage Units and RV Spaces.
                     • Maintaining Property Grounds.
                     • Bookkeeping.

                     1994 – 1996 Saddle West Hotel & Casino   Las Vegas, NV
                     Keno Shift Manager
                     • Swing Shift Supervisor.
                     • Organizing Special Events and Promotions.
                     • Training New Keno Hosts.

Education   2004   A.A. Paralegal Studies, University of Montana   Missoula, MT
                     • Substantive Course Family Law
                     • Substantive Course Contract Law

Computer Skills • Lexis, Microsoft and Excel Software

FIGURE 5.2

5926 Cypress Court   415.555.4356
San Francisco, CA 94143   LaceyPatten@cox.net

Lacey M. Patten

Objective   To obtain a paralegal position as a bilingual speaker including drafting pleadings, discovery, and motions and utilizing excellent computer processing skills, including proficiency in Windows, Word, Excel 1 & 2, PowerPoint, Lotus, WESTLAW and Lexis-Nexis.

Experience   2003 – 2004   ***Universal Fidelity Corporation***   *San Francisco, CA*
Administrative Assistant, Collections Department
- *Administrative Assistant, Collections Department.* Coordinated efforts of local managers to provide consistent business and reporting practices.
- *Supervisor, Large Balance Collectors.* Used computer system to track progress of large collections and followed up with issues where necessary.
- *Records Clerk, Human Resources.* Responsible for filtering and distributing applicant information to regional and local offices.

2000 – 2002   ***Fairfield Resorts***   *Reno, NV*
Account Agent, Collections
- Responsible for over 500 accounts.
- Tracked account information and determined individualized collection system.
- Maintained accounts account collection information and determined efficacy of collection methods.
- Implemented intensive 10 week training course for new collectors.

1996 – 2000   ***Richy's Locker Mini Storage***   *Pahrump, NV*
Property Manager
- Leased storage units and recreational vehicle spaces.
- Maintained property grounds.
- Provided accounting and bookkeeping services.

1996 – 1998   ***Saddle West Hotel & Casino***   *Las Vegas, NV*
Keno Shift Manager
- Supervised 10 employees as swing shift supervisor.
- Organized special events and promotions.
- Trained new Keno hosts.

Education   2004   ***University of Montana***   *Missoula, MT*
A.A., Paralegal Studies
- Course studies in legal terminology, legal procedures, court structure
- Document preparation included pleadings, discovery, and motion practice
- Substantive courses in contract and family law

Computer Skills Lexis, Microsoft and Excel Software

FIGURE 5.3

This resume is too cluttered	

RICARDO CORTEZ

8907 BROOMFIELD DRIVE □ LAS VEGAS, NEVADA 89154

702.555.3192 OR 702.555.9688

RICARDOC21780@HOTMAIL.COM

> *Poorly worded, self-serving objective; describe what you can offer the employer*

OBJECTIVE : Seeking a challenging position as a Paralegal that will allow me to explore the opportunities that are available within the profession.

EDUCATION

University of Nevada, Las Vegas   **Las Vegas, Nevada 89154**

Paralegal Certificate   Graduated, 2004

□ Relevant coursework included studies in Family Law, Advocacy, Criminal Law, Nevada Practices and Procedures
□ Document preparation including pleadings, discovery, and motions

Community College of Southern Nevada   **Henderson, Nevada 89015**

Graduated with Associate of Arts in Political Science with Honors   Graduated, 2000
□ Course study focused on Political Science
□ Graduated three months early

> *Not necessary to comment on early graduation*

> *Provide only the city/state*

LEGAL EXPERIENCE:

University of Nevada, Las Vegas Paralegal Continuing   **Las Vegas, Nevada 89154**

Education Program   Graduated, 2006

Paralegal Studies   October, 2004 to December, 2004
□ Researched laws, investigated facts and prepared documents in order to gain knowledge in assisting attorneys.
□ Performed mock settlement hearings and created mock client files which required the gathering/creation of evidence, pleadings, discovery documents, correspondence, legal research, forms such as background sheets and witness interviewing forms in divorce, civil, criminal and other cases in order to formulate defenses and initiate legal actions.
□ Wrote, designed and produced legal documents.
□ Prepared legal briefs, pleadings, appeals, developed strategies, arguments and testimony in preparation for presentation of case.
□ Researched and analyzed law sources such as statutes, recorded judicial decisions, legal articles, treaties, constitutions and legal codes.
□ Successfully handled settlement conferences.
□ Structured and maintained a client file.
□ Prepared affidavits of documents and maintained document files.
□ Learned how to deliver and direct subpoenas to witnesses and parties to action.

> *This section provides too much detail because it is repetitive; include only two or three descriptive sentences*

EXPERIENCE :

Committee to re-elect Senator Jack   **240 South Water Street**

Henderson, Nevada 89015

702.555.2323

Campaign Office Manager/Administrative Assistant   August, 2001 to Present
□ Oversaw internal public relations and media relations efforts
□ Participated in the creation of fundraising programs and event coordination
□ Performed miscellaneous general office tasks and managerial tasks (i.e. ran errands, answered telephones, scheduled meetings, and filed proposals, meeting notes, etc.)

> *Provide only the city/state*

720 West Sunrise Road

The Auto Title Loan Store   **Henderson, Nevada 89015**

March, 2003 to April, 2004

Store Manager
□ Responsible for debt collection leading up to and including small claims lawsuits for losses resulting from defaulted loans
□ Maintained client base of over 2,000 customers and coordinated store marketing efforts including networking with other local businesses

1301 West Sunrise Road

Sunset Station Hotel and Casino   **Henderson, Nevada 89014**

April, 1998 to March 2003

Host/Cashier/Server/Greeter/Trainer
□ Afforded significant exposure to guest relations and was frequently called upon to resolve customer and employee relation conflicts
□ Required to perform multiple tasks while maintaining excellent guest service in a large volume restaurant

FIGURE 5.4

RICARDO CORTEZ

8907 BROOMFIELD DRIVE □ LAS VEGAS, NEVADA 89154
702.555.3192 OR 702.555.9688
RICARDOC21780@HOTMAIL.COM

OBJECTIVE :
Seeking a challenging position in the paralegal profession.

EDUCATION:

University of Nevada, Las Vegas   *Las Vegas, Nevada*

Paralegal Certificate   *Graduated, 2006*

□ Relevant coursework included studies in Family Law, Advocacy, Criminal Law, Nevada Practices and Procedures
□ Document preparation including pleadings, discovery, and motions

Community College of Southern Nevada   *Henderson, Nevada*

Associate of Arts, Political Science with Honors   *Graduated, 2000*

LEGAL EXPERIENCE:

University of Nevada, Las Vegas   *Las Vegas, Nevada*

Paralegal Studies Certificate Program   *Graduated, 2006*

□ Performed mock settlement hearings and created mock client files which required the gathering/creation of evidence, pleadings, discovery documents, correspondence, legal research, forms such as background sheets and witness interviewing forms in divorce, civil, criminal and other cases to formulate defenses and initiate legal actions.
□ Prepared briefs, pleadings, appeals, developed strategies, arguments and testimony for case.
□ Researched and analyzed law sources such as statutes, recorded judicial decisions, legal articles, treaties, constitutions and legal codes.
□ Drafted legal documents.
□ Structured and maintained mock client file.
□ Prepared affidavits of documents and maintained document files.
□ Studied procedure for delivery and direction of subpoenas to witnesses and parties to action.

WORK EXPERIENCE:

Committee to re-elect Senator Jack Clark   Henderson, Nevada

Campaign Office Manager/Administrative Assistant   2001 to Present

□ Responsible for oversight of internal public relations and media relations efforts.
□ Participated in the creation of fundraising programs and event coordination.
□ Performed miscellaneous general office tasks and managerial tasks (e.g. ran errands, answered telephones, scheduled meetings, filed proposals, recorded meeting notes).

The Auto Title Loan Store   Henderson, Nevada

Store Manager   2003 to 2004

□ Responsible for debt collection leading up to and including small claims lawsuits for losses resulting from defaulted loans.
□ Maintained client base of over 2,000 customers and coordinated store marketing efforts including networking with other local businesses.

Sunset Station Hotel and Casino   Henderson, Nevada

Host /Cashier/Server/Greeter/ Trainer   1998 to 2003

□ Significant exposure to guest relations.
□ Frequently called upon to resolve customer and employee relation conflicts.
□ Performed multiple tasks while maintaining excellent guest service in large volume restaurant.

FIGURE 5.5

> Great resume layout, but it needs some clarity to be added with bullets and formatting

> This person owns the store; she should say so!

> Do not say "depending on the situation"

> Not necessary to give a reason for leaving

> Provide detail about the skills learned and documents prepared

> Shorten this listing and provide more detail about work experience

> Not necessary

Laurie M. Driscoll
4567 Winksor Dr., Gainsville, FL 32611
352.555.4971 Home
lauriegreenvalleyschool@hotmail.com

Objective

To obtain a paralegal position to utilize my experience and education as well as provide an opportunity for professional growth based upon performance.

Experience

Manager / Administrative Assistant   2003 – Present
Sign Inventions, Gainsville, Florida
In charge of customer service, general office duties, human resources, middle management duties payroll, file maintenance, some accounting, and various other duties depending on the situation.

Manager / Travel Agent   1996 – 2003
Travel Inc., Fort Collins, Colorado
(dba as Carlson Travel, Green Hill Travel)
In charge of customer service, management, general office duties and upkeep, accounting, numerous other duties depending on the situation.
Reason for leaving: Agency Closed

Administrative Assistant (Sales) / Receptionist   1993 – 1995
Win2 Technologies, San Bernardino, California
In charge of customer service, phones, scheduling appointments, drafting letters, preparing for stock holders meetings, and numerous other office duties.
Reason for leaving: Relocated back to Las Vegas

Education

University of Florida
Certificate in Paralegal Studies 2005

Abilities

Strong organizational and interpersonal skills
Adept at both oral and written communication
Interact effectively with public
Demonstrated record of high performance standards, including
Attention to schedules, deadlines, budgets and quality work.
General office duties, Microsoft Word, proofreading experience

References

Available on request

FIGURE 5.6

Laurie M. Driscoll
4567 Winksor Dr., Gainsville, FL 32611
352.555.4971 Home
<u>lauriegreenvalleyschool@hotmail.com</u>

Objective

To obtain a paralegal position that will utilize my experience and education as well as provide an opportunity for professional growth based upon performance.

Experience

Owner / Manager   2003 – Present

  Sign Inventions, *Gainsville, Florida*

- Facilitated customer service relations, performed general office duties
- Performed accounting duties, including payroll and invoicing, budgeting
- Supervised and scheduled ten employees

Manager / Travel Agent   1996 – 2003

  Travel Inc., *Fort Collins, Colorado (dba Carlson Travel, Green Hill Travel)*

- Provided customer service
- Coordinated and scheduled domestic and international client travel

Administrative Assistant (Sales) / Receptionist   1993 – 1995

  Win2 Technologies, *San Bernardino, California*

- Performed clerical duties including scheduling appointments, answering phones, drafting letters, proofreading, and preparing documents required for stock holders meetings
- Extensive use of Microsoft Word

Education

  University of Florida

  Certificate in Paralegal Studies 2006

- Researched legal issues, drafted legal documents, prepared pleadings, summarized documents, organized trial notebooks, and interviewed clients
- Prepared contracts and considered issues surrounding breach of contract and remedies
- Drafted wills, trusts, and probate documents
- Studied family law issues including divorce, separation, custody, adoption, and guardianship proceedings
- Studied criminal law including classification of crimes, defenses, and criminal procedures

Abilities

- Strong organizational and interpersonal skills
- Adept at both oral and written communication
- Computer literacy with Microsoft Word
- Excellent proofreading skills

FIGURE 5.7

This person is very qualified, but you cannot tell this from his crammed resume. He wants to work as a paralegal until he goes to law school and will need to explain this in his cover letter

The layout needs to be reworked so the reader can scan the information quickly; job titles should be in bold, dates in italics

Shorten job descriptions and highlight portions relevant to work in the legal field

Be aware of tense agreement

Omit the detail to include all of these work experience listings; limit descriptions to two or three sentences

In general, provide work history for no more than 10 years

Educational background should be listed before the work experience if you hold a BA, BS, or above

Use italics to set off the information listed

These qualifications and credentials can support a two-page resume, but the information is too crammed as presented

---

MARCUS W. ROLEX
P. O. Box 908
Las Vegas, NV 89114
MWROLEX@ AOL.COM
702.555.9890

PROFESSIONAL EXPERIENCE:

Jul. 2001 – Present, Mirage Casino Hotel (MGM/Mirage)
Las Vegas, Nevada 89109

Casino Floor Supervisor
Supervised all major table games.
Selected as Corporate Diversity Champion.
Designed breakeven analysis for table games staffing.

Casino Accounting Manager
Responsible for the auditing and posting of daily casino revenue.
Responsible for the reporting and filing of the monthly and quarterly gaming taxes.
Directly managed a staff of 14 auditor and two staff accounts.
Responsible for the month end journal entries and posting to the General Ledger.
Responsible for preparation, of the daily operating report.
Design audit program for the new coinless and one card slot system.
Responsible for ensuring regulatory compliance.

Aug. 2000 – Jul. 2001, Primadonna Company (MGM/Mirage)
(31900 S. Las Vegas Blvd. Primm NV. 89019)
Senior Financial Analyst
Responsible for preparation of the daily operating report.
Responsible for preparing the daily and weekly cash report.
Assisted in the preparation of month end financial statements.
Prepare profit & loss statements for casino marketing events.
Prepare the monthly MD&A reports to corporate office.
Budgeted and forecasted for property mid-size hotel & casino.
Instrumental in the restructuring of the risk management office.
Administrator of tenant leases for 10 food outlets.

Feb. 1995 – Aug. 2000 Caesars Palace (Park Place Entertainment)
Las Vegas Nevada 89109
Pit Manager/Assistant Shift Manager 1998 – 2000
Directly supervised casino with 120 table games and 2000 slot machines.
Responsible for setting table game limits for new players.
Wrote schedule for the shift, for optimal use of personnel.
Completed annual operating budget for the table games department.

Floor Supervisor 1996 – 1998
Directly supervise, dealers and pit clerks.
Design staffing charts for pit clerks resulting in more efficient staffing with 20% fewer personnel.

1988 – 1995 United States Navy
Naval Air Station Oceana Virginia Beach, Virginia 89014
Naval Officer and Aviator flying the A-6 Intruder
Supervised the aircraft division, consisting of four branch officers, eight non-commissioned officers and seventy-eight enlisted personnel. Reporting directly to the maintenance officer.

Schedule writer responsible for the scheduling of 42 aircrew and 16 aircraft.
Legal Officer responsible for ensuring squadron compliance with the UCMJ.
Flight officer responsible for monitoring flight time and training of aircrews.
Responsible for rewriting squadron operations procedures manual.

1984 – 1988 Las Vegas Hilton
Las Vegas Nevada 89109
Dice Dealer

Education:
Masters of Business Administration (MBA), University of Nevada Las Vegas
Specializing in Managerial Finance and Accounting, May 1999

Bachelor of Science (BS), University of Nevada Las Vegas
Specializing in Hotel Administration, and Casino Management May 1987

Associate of Applied Science (AAS), Southern Nevada Community College
Hotel Administration, May 1984

Associate of Applied Science (AAS), Southern Nevada Community College
Casino Management, May 1984

Community Service:
- Selected to UNLV Harrah Hotel College Alumni Association Board of Directors.
- Mentor to students in Harrah Hotel College Mentor Program.
- Keynote Speaker at Harrah Hotel College "Be a Rebel Day" diversity recruitment program.
- Guest speaker at area High Schools about the importance of higher education.
- Member of the Mirage Casino Hotel Employee Scholarship Committee.
- Member of the Mirage Casino Hotel Employee Emergency Relief Fund Committee.

FIGURE 5.8

MARCUS W. ROLEX
P. O. Box 908
Las Vegas, NV 89114
MWROLEX@AOL.COM
702.555.9890

EDUCATION:

2006   Certificate, Paralegal Studies
University of Nevada, Las Vegas
- Substantive coursework: Business Organizations and Contracts

1999   M.B.A., Business Administration
University of Nevada, Las Vegas
- Emphasis, Managerial Accounting

1987   B.S., Bachelor of Science
University of Nevada Las Vegas
- Emphasis, Hotel Administration and Casino Management

1984   A.A.S., Associate of Applied Science
Southern Nevada Community College
- Emphasis, Hotel Administration

1984   A.A.S., Associate of Applied Science
Southern Nevada Community College
- Emphasis, Casino Management

PROFESSIONAL EXPERIENCE:

Casino Floor Supervisor   *2003 – Present*
Mirage Casino Hotel (MGM/Mirage); Las Vegas, Nevada
- Supervised all major table games
- Selected as Corporate Diversity Champion
- Designed breakeven analysis for table games staffing

Casino Accounting Manager   *2001 – 2003*
Mirage Casino Hotel (MGM/Mirage); Las Vegas, Nevada
- Audited and posted daily casino revenue
- Reported and filed monthly and quarterly gaming taxes
- Directly managed auditors and accounting staff
- Recorded month end journal entries and posted to General Ledger
- Preparation daily operating report
- Designed audit program for the new coinless and one card slot system
- Ensured regulatory compliance

Senior Financial Analyst   *August 2000 – July 2001*
Primadonna Company (MGM/Mirage); Primm, Nevada
- Prepared daily operating reports
- Prepared daily and weekly cash reports
- Assisted in the preparation of month end financial statements
- Prepared profit & loss statements for casino marketing events
- Prepare the monthly MD&A reports to corporate office
- Budgeting and forecasting for property mid-size hotel & casino
- Instrumental in the restructuring of the risk management office
- Administrator of tenant leases for 10 food outlets

Pit Manager   *1998 – 2000*
Caesars Palace (Park Place Entertainment); Las Vegas, Nevada
- Directly supervised casino
- Set table game limits for new players
- Scheduled personnel for shifts
- Wrote annual operating budget for the table games department

Floor Supervisor   *1995 – 1998*
Caesars Palace (Park Place Entertainment); Las Vegas, Nevada
- Directly supervised dealers and pit clerks
- Redesigned staffing resulting in more efficient staffing with 20% fewer personnel

Naval Officer and Aviator   *1988 – 1995*
United States Navy; Virginia Beach, Virginia
- Supervised the aircraft division
- Scheduled aircrew and aircraft
- Legal Officer ensured squadron compliance with the UCMJ
- Flight Officer monitored flight time and training of aircrews
- Rewrote squadron operations procedures manual

COMMUNITY SERVICE:
- Selected to UNLV Harrah Hotel College Alumni Association Board of Directors
- Mentor to students in Harrah Hotel College Mentor Program
- Keynote Speaker at Harrah Hotel College "Be a Rebel Day" diversity recruitment program
- Guest speaker at area High Schools about the importance of higher education
- Member of the Mirage Casino Hotel Employee Scholarship Committee
- Member of the Mirage Casino Hotel Employee Emergency Relief Fund Committee

FIGURE 5.9

Most employers do not want to continue the applicant's education; they want to know what you can do for them

Professional summary is useful but it focuses primarily on non-legal experience

This is a good listing but the legal section should be shortened

Poor layout

Past tense is more appropriate for past employment

Verb tense agreement problems

This resume should be shortened by using job listings and providing minimal descriptions

7340 W. Serendity Rd. # 1080 Davis, California 95616

(530) 555-1652 E-Mail melindalopez99@yahoo.com

Melinda Lopez

Objective

To obtain a permanent position with a professional and well-structured company allowing me to continue my legal education, insurance, medical, and accounting experience.

Professional Summary

UNLV certified Paralegal familiar with document production, including pleadings, discovery and motions. Four years of accounting experience in accounts payables and receivables and familiar with accounting procedures and auditing. Six years of extensive medical experience in different areas such as Dialysis, Pharmaceutical, D.M.E, Physician, and collections and billing for Medicare, Medicaid, HMO, PPO, POS, Culinary, Cobra and Workers-Comp. Overall knowledge of general insurance procedures including various aspects of medical, life, property, and casualty.

Skills Summary

Operating systems/Software: 50 WPM and ten key by touch -Windows, Word, Excel 1 & 2, PowerPoint, Lotus, Medical Manager, Med Act, Peachtree, Platinum ERA, Proton, TDH Connect, Medifax, OAS gold, Tiger, Misys, Argon, MAS 90 & 200, WESTLAW and Lexis.

Language: Fluent in Spanish

Medical: ICD-9, CPT coding, and auditing

Legal: Legal research, legal writing, citation form, ethical considerations, form preparation, legal terminology, interviewing, investigation, analysis, pleadings, discovery preparation, file maintenance and deposition digesting, and settlement conference preparation.

Work Experience

2003 – Present   JTI, International   Sacramento, California

Accounts Payable/Contract Paralegal (Promoted 3/2004)

- In charge of accounts payable for two local companies, one hospital and four clinics in California.
- Handle all financial accounts payable invoices to be paid in a timely manner.

Collector/Billing Specialist (04/2003-03/2004)

- Billing and collection services for hospitals, clinics and Physician offices to include Nevada and California Workers Compensation, Medi-Cal, Culinary, Commercial and self pay.

2001 – 2003   Fresno Medical Care   San Antonio, Texas

Insurance Coordinator/Admissions Trainer

- Retrieving insurance referrals/prior authorizations, verifying eligibility for 24 End-Stage Renal Disease freestanding clinics in Texas.
- Training employees in Medical procedures and guidelines for coordinating medical insurance.
- Approving patient forms and files for completion.
- Filing, date entry, company accounts payable monthly invoices.

2000 – 2001   Summit D.M.E   San Antonio, Texas

Billing/Collections Specialist

- Processing of verification, registrations and authorizations of commercial and workers-comp claims for durable medical equipment.
- Confirmed medical delivery tickets for Hospice home healthcare patients.
- Resolved complex insurance related issues including interpreting EOB's, denial appealing, collections, adjustments and write offs.
- Maintaining continual performance in retrieval of funds as set by company standards and goals. Active retrieval of funds on delinquent aging and current accounts.

1999 – 2000   Pro-Mark Pharmacies   San Antonio, Texas

Accounting Executive to CEO

- Responsible for daily accounts receivable deposits, accounts payable, preparation of billing statements and workers-comp claims.
- Assisting in company finance procedures. Preparing monthly reports and correspondence.
- Customer Service representative assigned to resolve patient accounts and payables.

Education

2004   **University of California, Davis** A.A. in Paralegal Studies with emphasis in California Practices and Procedures, Family Law, Contract Law and Hospitality Law (HIPPA) Trained

"Physician **Risk Areas and Compliance Program**"

Certified Excel Level 1 & 2

Rockhurst University-Certificate for Organizing & Managing Accounts Payable, Handling Difficult and Demanding Customers, and Use and Sales Tax.

Member of the Institute of Internal Auditors-Las Vegas Nevada Chapter

2001   **Professional Association of Healthcare Office Managers**-Completed Billing course

1999   **Group 01-01 Legal Reserve Life Insurance Agent**- License training 120 hours

FIGURE 5.10

Melinda Lopez

7340 W. Serendity Rd. # 1080   (530) 555-1652
Davis, California 95616   melindalopez99@yahoo.com

Objective

To obtain a permanent position with a professional organization allowing me to utilize my legal education, as well as my insurance, medical, and accounting experience.

Skills Summary

Computer: 50 WPM and ten key by touch -Windows, Word, Excel 1 & 2, PowerPoint, Lotus, Medical Manager, Med Act, Peachtree, Platinum ERA, Proton, TDH Connect, Medifax, OAS gold, Tiger, Misys, Argon, MAS 90 & 200, WESTLAW and Lexis.

Language: Fluent in Spanish

Medical: ICD-9, CPT coding, and auditing

Legal: Legal research and writing, citation form, ethics, form preparation, interviewing, investigation, analysis, pleadings, discovery preparation, file maintenance and depositions, and settlements.

Education

2004   **University of California, Davis** A.A., Paralegal Studies
- Emphasis in California Practices and Procedures, Family Law, Contract Law and Hospitality Law

2003   **"Physician Risk Areas and Compliance Program"**
- Certified Excel Level 1 & 2

2002   **Rockhurst University**
- Certification, Organizing & Managing Accounts Payable, Handling Difficult and Demanding Customers, and Use and Sales Tax.

2001   **Professional Association of Healthcare Office Managers**
- Billing course

1999   **Group 01-01 Legal Reserve Life Insurance Agent**
- License training 120 hours

Work Experience

JTI International; *Sacramento, California*   *2003 – Present*
Accounts Payable/Contract Paralegal (2004)
- Accounts payable for local companies, hospitals and clinics.
Collector/Billing Specialist (2003- 2004)
- Provided billing and collection services for hospitals.

Fresno Medical Care; *San Antonio, Texas*   *2001 – 2003*
Insurance Coordinator/Admissions Trainer
- Processed insurance referrals/prior authorizations and eligibility.
- Provided approval of patient forms and files; assisted with social work.

Summit D.M.E.: *San Antonio, Texas*   *2000 – 2001*
Billing/Collections Specialist
- Processed verification, registrations and authorizations for medical equipment.
- Resolved complex insurance related issues. Responsible for retrieval on delinquent aging & current accounts.

Pro-Mark Pharmacies; *San Antonio, Texas*   *1999 – 2000*
Accounting Executive to CEO
- Worked on accounts payable, receivable, billing statements, monthly reports, workers-comp claims and related accounting issues.

FIGURE 5.11

PEGGY A. AMAHD

9309 Sien Ridge Drive   Home: (907) 555-7611
Anchorage, Alaska 99516   Cell: (907) 555-9812

HotPeggy@aol.com

Yikes!! This email address is not professional

OBJECTIVE:

To obtain a part-time entry level position in the legal field with potential to utilize my current and past experience.

Describe the experience; this is too vague. Also, you may get an entry-level position, but don't ask for one

EDUCATION:

Associate of Applied Science, Paralegal Studies, 2007
University of Cincinnati, Ohio
  - General studies in preparation for paralegal career including ethical considerations, legal research, legal writing, citation form, interviewing, law office investigation, pleading preparation, coordination of discovery, basics of arbitration, form preparation.
  - Program included specific substantive courses in Family Law and Constitutional Law.

General Studies, 1999 – 2003
Community College of Southern Alaska, Juneau, Alaska

She also has her paralegal certificate and should mention this

RELEVANT SKILLS:

Microsoft Office; typing 70 w.p.m; shorthand 100 w.p.m.
Detail oriented, self-starter, motivated, organized

WORK HISTORY:

1998 – Present	Part-time student; full-time homemaker
1994 – 1998	Volunteer - Johnson Middle School and Piggott Elementary Schools, Las Vegas, Nevada Supervised students in management of student store; Member PTA; Organized and planned numerous school programs; reading tutor
	Volunteer - Peccole Little League, Las Vegas, Nevada Operated snack bar; team mom
Prior Positions	Office manager, clerical supervisor, secretary, medical unit coordinator, medical records file clerk

Clearly a "Stay-at-Home Mom" resume. This resume should list her several volunteer positions with the school separately,with creative job titles for each

The spacing is off and the layout should use bold and italics for emphasis

Provide a listing with details of previous positions; years may be omitted

ACTIVITIES/INTERESTS:

Reading, downhill skiing, hiking, home decorating

Interests can be listed as a "space filler" but otherwise are frowned upon; interests such as home decorating probably should not be included

FIGURE 5.12

PEGGY A. AMAHD

9309 Sien Ridge Drive
Anchorage, Alaska 99516

Home: (907) 555-7611
Cell: (907) 555-9812
E-Mail: **peggyamahdlegal@aol.com**

OBJECTIVE:

To obtain a part-time position in the legal field with potential to utilize my paralegal education and my strong organizational and computer skills.

EDUCATION:

Associate of Applied Science, Paralegal Studies, 2005
University of Cincinnati, Ohio
- General studies in preparation for paralegal career included ethical considerations, legal research, legal writing, citation form, interviewing, law office investigation, pleading preparation, coordination of discovery, basics of arbitration, form preparation.
- Program included specific substantive courses in Family Law and Constitutional Law.

General Studies, 1999 – 2002
Community College of Southern Alaska, Juneau, Alaska

RELEVANT SKILLS:

Microsoft Office: Word, Excel, PowerPoint; typing 70 WPM; shorthand 100 WPM

WORK EXPERIENCE:

1994 – 2000

Student Store Manager   *Johnson Middle School – Volunteer*   *Las Vegas, Nevada*
Supervised students in the management of a student store, including inventory management, cash register skills, and basic accounting.

Book Bowl Coach/Coordinator   *Piggott Elementary School – Volunteer*   *Las Vegas, Nevada*
Book Bowl parent coach (3 years) and coordinator (1 year). Worked with groups of students and organized parents to help students analyze literary works culminating in a student team competition.

Read-A-Thon Coordinator   *Piggott Elementary School – Volunteer*   *Las Vegas, Nevada*
Coordinated guest readers, pledges for students, prizes, advertising and all other aspects of the PTA's major fundraiser, the annual Read-A-Thon.

Reading Tutor   *Piggott Elementary School – Volunteer*   *Las Vegas, Nevada*
Helped struggling students develop reading skills by meeting one on one with students twice a week throughout the school year. Involved learning current strategies used by educators.

Team Mom   *Little League, Volunteer*   *Las Vegas, Nevada*
Organized team by taking care of administrative details such as snack schedules, end of season coach gifts, team photos.

Prior to 1994:

Office Manager
Management of office staff, computer system, and accounting projects.

Clerical Supervisor
Supervised operations of staff hiring and scheduling and customer support.

Medical Unit Coordinator
Transcribed doctors' orders, scheduled tests/treatments, maintained patients' charts, and managed supplies.

Medical Records File Clerk
Maintained health data by sorting and filing medical records and processing medical records.

FIGURE 5.13

This is very cluttered; it contains great information but it should be condensed

Lisa D. Lawless
5880 Boulder Drive, Charlotte, North Carolina 28223 704.555.9898

OBJECTIVE
A paralegal position that will benefit from initiative, organizational skills, excellent work ethic, and multi-tasking abilities.

EDUCATION

B.S., Criminal Justice   *1998*
University of Colorado, Boulder, Colorado - *Cum Laude*

CERTIFICATIONS
- **Paralegal Certificate,** University of North Carolina, Charlotte 2006
- **Certified Washroom Technician,** National Association of Institutional Linen Management, 2004
- **Certified Laundry and Linen Manager,** National Association of Institutional Linen Management, 2003

The last two certifications should be omitted as irrelevant

Shorten the skills section based upon transferable skills

SKILLS
- Extensive experience in analytical and technical work. Researched state and federal laws to ensure compliance with health & safety regulations, and various other programs.
- Well-organized, efficient, dependable, and conscientious. Detail-oriented, ability to multi-task, and work effectively in a constantly changing environment.
- Computer literate, proficient in Windows, MS Word, Outlook, familiar with Excel and Access.
- Excellent interpersonal, written and verbal communication skills.

EXPERIENCE

Inmate Employability Coordinator   *2003 to 2004*
State of N.C. - Prison Industry Authority, Raleigh, N.C. - A local representative responsible for documenting and assisting inmates to obtain the necessary skills for employment upon release from prison, through written evaluations, counseling, certification programs, resume preparation, and interviewing skills.
- Established certification programs on Communication, Decision Making, and Haz-Mat through FEMA, now being used throughout the State at 23 institutions.
- Issued over 200 certificates and licenses through, FEMA, National Association of Institutional Management, and Electronic Technician Association.

Industrial Supervisor   *2001 to 2003*
State of N.C. - Prison Industry Authority, Raleigh, N.C. - Plan and schedule production including labor, materials, and equipment. Train, counsel, and supervise incarcerated individuals on production, quality control, and safety. Maintain security of work areas through searches for contraband.
- Work with customers to ensure laundry is processed timely and efficiently while maintaining quality control.
- Order supplies, maintain budget, production, maintenance, and inventory records. Create Capital Equipment Justifications and Requests. Process all inmate time keeping and payroll records.
- Established a local Health & Safety Program, including an Injury Illness and Prevention Program, and new hire orientation on safety, policies, and procedures.

Management Services Technician   *1999 to 2001*
State of CA - Prison Industry Authority, Folsom, CA - Involved with all aspects of customer service to the public and government agencies.

She is changing tense between sections

Shorten the job descriptions and emphasize programs established by the applicant

FIGURE 5.14

Lisa D. Lawless

5880 Boulder Drive, Charlotte, North Carolina 28223   704.555.9898

OBJECTIVE

A paralegal position in a law firm which will benefit from initiative, organizational skills, excellent work ethic, and multi-tasking abilities.

EDUCATION

Paralegal Studies Certificate   *2006*

University of North Carolina, Charlotte

B.S., Criminal Justice   *1998*

University of Colorado, Boulder, Colorado Cum Laude

SKILLS

- Extensive experience in analytical and technical work. Research experience with state and federal laws for compliance with Health & Safety regulations and associated programs.
- Well-organized, efficient, dependable, detail-oriented and conscientious.
- Proficient in Windows, MS Word, Outlook, familiar with Excel and Access.

EXPERIENCE

Inmate Employability Coordinator   *2003 to 2004*

State of North Carolina. - Prison Industry Authority, Raleigh, N.C.

- Responsible for documenting and assisting inmates to obtain the necessary skills for employment upon release from prison, through written evaluations, counseling, certification programs, resume preparation, and interviewing skills.

  ➤ *Established certification programs for Communication, Decision Making, and Haz-Mat through FEMA. Certifications, now being used throughout North Carolina at 23 institutions.*

Industrial Supervisor   *2001 to 2003*

State of North Carolina - Prison Industry Authority, Raleigh, N.C.

- Planned and scheduled production including labor, materials, and equipment. Trained, counseled, and supervised incarcerated individuals on production, quality control, and safety. Maintained security of work areas through contraband searches.
- Ordered supplies, maintained budget, production, maintenance, and inventory records.
- Processed all inmate time keeping and payroll records.

  ➤ *Established a local Health & Safety Program, including Injury Illness and Prevention Program, and New Hire Orientation covering safety, policies, and procedures.*

Management Services Technician   *1999 to 2001*

State of California - Prison Industry Authority, Folsom, CA

Coordinated customer service to the public and government agencies.

FIGURE 5.15

Nice layout

The same fonts should be used throughout

The objective provides no information to the employer

Good, boldinghighlights job responsibilities

Did she just attend the program or did she receive the certificate?

Shannon R. Bormen

3638 Sunshine Road, Las Vegas, NV 89120
Phone: 702.555.3308   Cell: 702.555.9841

Objective/Profile

My objective is to work in a dynamic environment with supportive management and co-workers that allows me to use my knowledge and skills in a growing, productive career. I am self-motivated, highly organized and resourceful. I enjoy challenges and new endeavors and am able to take the initiative to meet goals.

Experience

2005 – 2005   **UNLV PARALEGAL PROGRAM;** *Las Vegas, NV*
Student
Completing certificate course in paralegal studies at UNLV with substantive courses of Business Law, Criminal Law, and Tort Law.

2003 – 2004   **MGM GRAND SPA AT MIRAGE HOTEL;** *Las Vegas, NV*
Massage Therapist
Performing various modalities of massage and spa therapies including Swedish, Shiatsu, deep tissue, trigger point, reflexology, hot rock, body wraps and salt glows.

2003 – 2003   **DAHAN INSTITUTE OF MASSAGE STUDIES;** *Las Vegas, NV*
Marketing/Administration

Responsible for market development, public relations and sales initiatives for the growth of the company, including event scheduling, coordination, setup and personally representing the company at all events; the development and procurement of all marketing materials; lead generation and follow-up, appointment setting and student enrollment and admissions process.

1997 – 2003   **CITY OF HENDERSON;** *Henderson, NV*
Police Officer
All police officer duties, including basic POST certification and training in firearms, community policing, emergency vehicle operations, crime scene preservation, property seizure and forfeiture, custodial interference, domestic violence, defensive tactics, courtroom procedures and demeanor, arrest law, incident command, mobile field force, verbal judo, internal investigations, handling and maintenance of warrants, defibrillation, CPR and first aid.

Computer Literacy

- Lexis-Nexis
- Word
- Excel
- Access
- PowerPoint
- Outlook
- 10-Key
- Video Editing
- Photoshop
- Worldwide Web

Education

1/05 – 5/05   **UNLV Paralegal Program**   Las Vegas, NV
Student

- Legal Research
- Legal Writing
- Nevada Practices and Procedure
- Business Law
- Criminal Law
- Tort Law

FIGURE 5.16

Shannon R. Bormen

3638 Sunshine Road, Las Vegas, NV 89120
Phone: 702.555.3308 Cell: 702.555.9841

Objective/Profile

My objective is to obtain a paralegal position that allows me to use my knowledge and skills in a growing, productive career. I offer extensive experience in a variety of computer programs, including WORD, Excel, Access, PowerPoint, Outlook, and Photoshop. I am extremely self-motivated and able to work independently.

Experience

2007   *UNLV PARALEGAL PROGRAM*   Las Vegas, NV
Student
- Paralegal studies including legal terminology, court structure, legal procedures
- Emphasis in Business Law, Criminal Law, and Tort Law.

2003 – 2004   *MGM GRAND SPA AT MIRAGE HOTEL*   Las Vegas, NV
Massage Therapist
- Performed various modalities of massage including Swedish, Shiatsu, deep tissue
- Spa therapies trigger point, reflexology, hot rock, body wraps and salt glows.

2003 – 2003   *DAHAN INSTITUTE OF MASSAGE STUDIES*   Las Vegas, NV
Marketing/Administration
- Provided market development, public relations and sales initiatives
- Coordinated event scheduling
- Developed student enrollment and admissions process.

1997 – 2003   *CITY OF HENDERSON*   Henderson, NV
Police Officer
- Performed police officer duties, including basic POST certification and training in firearms, community policing, emergency vehicle operations, crime scene preservation, property seizure and forfeiture, custodial interference, domestic violence, defensive tactics, courtroom procedures and demeanor, arrest law, incident command, mobile field force, verbal judo, internal investigations, handling and maintenance of warrants, defibrillation, CPR and first aid.

Computer Literacy

- Lexis-Nexis
- Word
- Excel
- Access
- PowerPoint

- Outlook
- 10-Key
- Video Editing
- Photoshop
- Worldwide Web

Education

1/05 – 5/05   **UNLV Paralegal Certificate**   Las Vegas, NV

- Legal Research
- Legal Writing
- Nevada Practices and Procedure

- Business Law
- Criminal Law
- Tort Law

FIGURE 5.17

Notice e-mail address

This resume needs more variety to help highlight his qualifications

Redundant to note the time period and state it in the descriptive section

Bullets should be used to highlight experience

It is not necessary to state that these are available; the employer will ask if he or she wants to review either of these

JERRY CORVETT

hotcorvette@cox.net
530-555-4223

790 West Gilmore Ave
Davis, California 95616

EDUCATION

2006
Paralegal Certificate, University of California, Davis

- General studies in preparation for paralegal career included ethical considerations, legal research, legal writing, citation form, interviewing, law office investigation, pleading preparation, coordination of discovery and basics of arbitration.
- Program included specific substantive courses in Family Law and Constitutional Law.

1988
Bachelor of Arts, University of Miami

- Major, Political Science
- Studies included government structure, comparative government, judicial processes, political theory, logic, statistics.

WORK EXPERIENCE

1991 – Present
Food Server, Palace Station Casino

- Employed for thirteen years as a Food Server. To be successful in this fast-paced, high-pressure environment, many skills must be utilized. These skills include time management as I coordinate service to the customer; prioritizing of tasks to insure prompt service; highly effective communication as I talk to a vast demographic range of customers and delegate tasks to subordinates; extreme organization as I handle a multiplicity of duties. Successful implementation of these skills ensure that I will thrive in this environment.

SKILLS

- Advanced proficiency in Microsoft Word, Excel, and Outlook.
- Learning Photoshop and FrontPage presently.

References and writing samples available.

FIGURE 5.18

JERRY CORVETT

jerrycorvett@cox.net

530.555.1212

790 West Gilmore Ave

Davis, California 95616

OBJECTIVE

To obtain a position as a paralegal which will utilize my education as well as my time management, communication, and organizational skills.

EDUCATION

2006

Paralegal Certificate, University of California, Davis

- General studies in preparation for paralegal career included ethical considerations, legal research, legal writing, citation form, interviewing, law office investigation, pleading preparation, coordination of discovery, basics of arbitration, form preparation.

- Program included specific substantive courses in Family Law and Constitutional Law.

1988

Bachelor of Arts, University of Miami

- Major, Political Science
- Studies included government structure, comparative government, judicial processes, political theory, logic, statistics.

WORK EXPERIENCE

1991 – Present   **Food Server, Palace Station Casino**

Successful employee in high-paced service industry. Skills developed include:
- Time management coordinating service to the customer.
- Prioritizing of tasks to insure prompt service.
- Highly effective communication skills in dealing with vast demographic range of customers.
- Organization in coordinating multiple customer orders simultaneously.

COMPUTER SKILLS

- Advanced proficiency in Microsoft Word, Excel, and Outlook.
- Familiarity with Photoshop and FrontPage.

FIGURE 5.19

This is a good generic objective, particularly as she notes that she has 15 years of experience as a paralegal

Use bullets instead of narrative

Note that her listed experience does not support this section

The reference to "Program" suggests that she may not have received the certificate

E. NOEMY LAREZ

3771 Rosetop Circle S.
Las Vegas, NV 89121

(702) 555-8900
noemylarez@hotmail.net

OBJECTIVE

Seeking a paralegal position in a law firm where my extensive experience, education, talents, and abilities are used effectively.

PERSONAL PROFILE

Offering over 15 years of experience in all aspects of personal injury law, bankruptcy, general civil litigation, and business transactions. Six years experience in office management, personnel training, supervision and motivation, public relations, corporate, and international environments.

SUMMARY OF QUALIFICATIONS

- *Coordinate daily operations and evaluate administrative procedure* to ensure accurate, efficient, total quality management. Prioritize and manage heavy workflow without direct supervision. Drafting of demand letters, complaints, various pleadings, memorandum of law for many different motions, arbitration and mediation briefs. Researched and briefed cases in personal injury, medical malpractice, premises liability, wrongful death, and bankruptcy.

- *Bilingual in English and Spanish*

PROFESSIONAL EXPERIENCE

1993 – 2004   LAW OFFICES OF ROBERT S. HOTMAN, INC. *Los Angeles, CA*
   Administrative/Litigation Secretary
   - Under attorney supervision, managed all phases of client files to final resolution. Developed business contacts, negotiated pre-litigation cases and medical lines.
   - Maintained office calendar and statutes of limitations.
   - Drafted various pleadings, motions, propounding and responding discovery, drafted and responding to office correspondence. Ensured quality control, completed all projects on time.

1985 – 1993 LAW OFFICES OF BRUCE D. LITTLE   *Los Angeles, CA*
   aka NATIONAL MARKETING
   Legal Assistant
   - Handling files in all aspects of pre-litigation stages from screening possible new personal injury cases.
   - Settling pre-litigation personal injury claims and medical liens.

EDUCATION

2004   *UNLV Paralegal Certificate Program*
   Training in terminology, ethics, legal writing & research, interviewing, investigation, analysis, citation form, pleading & discovery preparation, file maintenance, deposition digesting, and Nevada Practices & Procedures.

FIGURE 5.20

E. NOEMY LAREZ

3771 Rosetop Circle S.   (702) 555-8900
Las Vegas, NV 89121   noemylarez@hotmail.net

OBJECTIVE

Seeking a paralegal position in a law firm where my 15 years of experience as a litigation paralegal, as well as my, education, talents, and abilities are used effectively.

PERSONAL PROFILE

Offering over 15 years of experience in all aspects of *personal injury law, bankruptcy, general civil litigation, and business transactions*.

SUMMARY OF QUALIFICATIONS

- Coordinate daily operations and evaluate administrative procedure to ensure accurate, efficient, total quality management.
- Prioritize and manage heavy workflow without direct supervision.
- Drafting of demand letters, complaints, various pleadings, memorandum of law for many different motions, arbitration and mediation briefs.
- Researched and briefed cases in personal injury, medical malpractice, premises liability, wrongful death, and bankruptcy.

- ***Bilingual in English and Spanish***

PROFESSIONAL EXPERIENCE

1993 – 2004   LAW OFFICES OF ROBERT S. HOTMAN, INC.   *Los Angeles, CA*
              Administrative/Litigation Secretary
              - Under attorney supervision, managed all phases of client files to final resolution. Developed business contacts, negotiated pre-litigation cases and medical lines.
              - Maintained office calendar and monitored statutes of limitations.
              - Drafted various pleadings, motions, propounding and responding to discovery, drafted and responding to office correspondence. Ensured quality control, completed all projects on time.

1985 – 1993   LAW OFFICES OF BRUCE D. LITTLE   *Los Angeles, CA*
              aka NATIONAL MARKETING
              Legal Assistant
              - Handled files in all aspects of pre-litigation stages from screening possible new personal injury cases.
              - Settled pre-litigation personal injury claims and medical liens.

EDUCATION

2004   **UNLV Paralegal Certificate**
              Training in terminology, ethics, legal writing and research, interviewing, investigation, analysis, citation form, pleading and discovery preparation, file maintenance, deposition digesting, and substantive training in Nevada Practices & Procedures, Litigation, Contract Law, HOA Law and Bankruptcy.

FIGURE 5.21

> *This is a vague and boring objective! She needs to list some of her qualifications*

> *Emphasize experience that will be valuable to a legal career (e.g., managed 30 first-grade students; prepared daily lesson plans and schedule)*

> *Phone numbers are not necessary; she should plan on providing a reference list at the interview*

> *The font choice is awkward. Choose Times New Roman and use bold and italics for emphasis, rather than changing font styles and sizes*

> *An on-line portfolio of legal work/projects is a great plus*

Brenda Kayge
564 Shale Circle
Stanton, New York 10003
212.555.8948
brenda@accessorycom.com

Objective

A paralegal position that will utilize my abilities developed through my education and experience.

Professional Experience

- Sylvan Learning Center; Stanton, New York; 212.555.9023
  Tutor, August 2003 – Present
    - Tutor Reading, Math, Writing, and Study Skills

- Stanton County School District; Stanton, New York; 212.569.5011
  Teacher, May 2002 – August 2003
    - Teach First Grade

- Advanced Micropolish Inc; Fremont, California; 510.555.4900
  Customer Product Manager, November 2000 – December 2001
    - Communicate with Engineering and Quality for pricing
    - Coordinate with Materials, Manufacturing and Shipping
    - Collaborate with AMI-Texas to serve customers in TX and CA

- KinderCare Center; Milpitas, California; 408.555.7212
  Assistant Director, January 2000 – September 2000
    - Operate center in Director's absence
    - Oversee curriculum implementation

- Crestwood Local School District; Mantua, Ohio; 330.555.8511
  Teacher, February 1994 - November 1999
    - Teach Title I Reading
    - Teach First Grade

Education

- UNC; Charlotte, NC
  Paralegal Certificate, May 2004

- Marygrove College; Detroit MI
  M.A., Teaching, December 1999

- Hiram College; Hiram OH
  B.A., Elementary Education, June 1993

Portfolio available at http://www.accesscom.com/~Kayge/brenda/portfolio/
References available upon request

FIGURE 5.22

Brenda Kayge
564 Shale Circle
Stanton, New York 10003
212.555.8948
brenda@accessorycom.com

Objective
> A paralegal position that will utilize my communication and organizational skills and allow for professional development within the legal field.

Professional Experience
Tutor, August 2003 – Present
Sylvan Learning Center; Stanton, New York
> Tutor reading, math, writing, and study skills

Teacher, May 2002 – August 2003
Stanton County School District; Stanton, New York
- Managed 22 first grade students
- Prepared daily lesson plans
- Collaborated with other primary teachers for scheduling and curriculum consistency
- Worked with wide range of students from special needs to gifted

Customer Product Manager, November 2000 – December 2001
Advanced Micropolish Inc; Fremont, California
- Communicated with Engineering and Quality for pricing
- Coordinated with Materials, Manufacturing and Shipping
- Collaborated with AMI-Texas to serve customers in TX and CA

Assistant Director, January 2000 – September 2000
KinderCare Center; Milpitas, California
- Operated center in Director's absence
- Oversaw curriculum implementation

Teacher, February 1994 – November 1999
Crestwood Local School District; Mantua, Ohio
- Taught Title I Reading
- Taught First Grade

Education
- University of North Carolina; Charlotte, NC
  Paralegal Certificate, May 2004

- Marygrove College; Detroit MI
  M.A., Teaching, December 1999

- Hiram College; Hiram OH
  B.A., Elementary Education, June 1993

FIGURE 5.23

> *Great qualifications but resume is too busy*

> *This should be condensed*

> *Fantastic listing of awards—this shows motivation and work achievement*

> *This section shows motivation*

ANGELIQUE DAN

381 Sany Way · Henderson, NV 89014 · angelique@people.com · (702) 555-7614

OBJECTIVE

Seeking a position in the **LEGAL FIELD,** where recent paralegal certification and proven customer relations, organizational, and multi-tasking skills will be effectively utilized and enhanced.

EDUCATION

UNIVERSITY of NEVADA, LAS VEGAS - Certificate: Paralegal Studies, 2004

QUALIFICATIONS

- Recent training in legal administration and paralegal studies encompassed Nevada Practices and Procedures, NRS, NAC, Rules of Evidence, legal research, writing, and litigation support.
- Practical knowledge of legal terminology; preparing discovery requests; and drafting and filing motions interrogatories, pleadings, and affidavits.
- Able to interview clients; schedule depositions and court reporters; summarize depositions, videotapes and medical records; and to assemble and organize files and exhibits for trial.
- Computer skills include Windows, MS Word, Excel, WordPerfect, Lexis-Nexis, and WESTLAW

EXPERIENCE

Account Manager; Credit Rejection, Henderson, Nevada
2002 – 2004
- ➢ Analyzed individual loans to determine potential risk of default on loan accounts. Resolved delinquent accounts and outstanding customer issues. Verified and updated account records.

Default Recovery / Prevention Representative; Smae, Las Vegas, Nevada
1998 – 2001
- ➢ Successfully motivated borrowers to resolve delinquent and defaulted student loans via phone, fax, and mail. Performed skip tracing and account documentation functions.
- ➢ *Consistently rated as one of the Top 10 of 300 Collectors. Achieved "Highest Quality Performer" for 1999. Named "Employee of the Month" in October 1999.*

Collections Specialist ; NRB, Las Vegas, Nevada
1997 – 1998
- ➢ Collected two to six month overdue monies from consumer department store accounts.
- ➢ Obtained actual collections in excess of $40,000 on a monthly basis.
- ➢ *Recognized as the "Top Collector" in Dec. 1997 and Jan. 1998.*
- ➢ *Received a "Team Player Award" in 1998.*

BUSINESS STUDIES

SALLIEMAE, LAS VEGAS, NV - **Business Ethics, Employment Law, Conflict Resolution, 1998-2001**
STEPHEN COVEY - **"Seven Habits of Highly Effective People" and "What Matters Most," 1998**

Figure 5.24

ANGELIQUE DAN

---

381 Sany Way · Henderson, NV 89014 · angelique@people.com · (702) 555-7614

OBJECTIVE

Seeking a position in the legal field, where recent paralegal certification and proven customer relations, organizational, and multi-tasking skills will be effectively utilized and enhanced.

EDUCATION

UNIVERSITY of NEVADA, LAS VEGAS   **Certificate: Paralegal** *Studies,* **2004**

- Researched legal issues, drafted legal documents, prepared pleadings, summarized documents, organized trial notebooks, and interviewed lients.
- Contracts including formation of contracts, breach of contracts, and remedies for breach of contracts.
- Estate planning, wills, trusts, estate taxes, estate sales, joint tenancy, and judicial determination of death.
- Family law including divorce, separation, custody, adoption, guardianship, and community property.
- Criminal law including defining common law, statutory crimes and punishment, classification of crimes, principles of liability by specific defenses, and basic criminal procedure concepts.

QUALIFICATIONS

- Legal administration and paralegal studies.
- Knowledge of legal terminology; preparing discovery requests; and drafting and filing motions interrogatories, pleadings, and affidavits.
- Computer skills include Windows, MS Word, Excel, WordPerfect, Lexis-Nexis, and WESTLAW

EXPERIENCE

Account Manager   Credit Rejection, Henderson, Nevada
2002 – 2004

➢ Analyzed individual loans to determine potential risk of default on loan accounts.
  Resolved delinquent accounts and outstanding customer issues. Verified and updated account records.

Default Recovery / Prevention Representative   Smae, Las Vegas, Nevada
1998 – 2001

➢ Successfully motivated borrowers to resolve delinquent and defaulted student loans via phone, fax, and mail. Performed skip tracing and account documentation functions.
➢ *Consistently rated as one of the Top 10 of 300 Collectors.*
➢ *Achieved "Highest Quality Performer" for 1999.*
➢ *Named "Employee of the Month" in October 1999.*

Collections Specialist   NRB, Las Vegas, NV
1997 – 1998

➢ Collected two to six month overdue monies from consumer department store accounts.
➢ Obtained actual collections in excess of $40,000 on a monthly basis.
➢ *Recognized as the "Top Collector" in December 1997 and January 1998.*
➢ *Received a "Team Player Award" in 1998.*

◉ Points to Consider

1. *Resume Format.* Choose a resume format from the samples provided in this chapter.

2. *Proofread.* Proofread your resume to catch spelling, grammar, and other errors. Run spelling and grammar checks and ask a friend or colleague to read your resume to check for errors or omissions.

3. *20-Second Rule.* Ask someone to glance at your resume for 20 seconds. After that time, ask the reader to write down four items she recalls from her review. If she cannot clearly identify four points, consider redrafting your resume to highlight your accomplishments more effectively.

◉ Job Search Tips

1. *Research Job Opportunities.* Research job opportunities available in your area. Consider whether your objective is sufficiently broad to encompass the majority of positions listed. Objectives that are written to cover only a narrow job market may limit your potential to get hired.

2. *Electronic Resume.* Identify those employers you intend to target in your application process. If the majority of your resume submissions will be on-line, create an electronic version of your resume. Instructions and a template for an electronic resume are provided in Chapter 10.

CHAPTER 6

INTRODUCING YOUR RESUME WITH A COVER LETTER

Your cover letter introduces you and your resume to an employer; think of it as your five-second Super Bowl commercial.

COVER LETTERS

- PERSONALIZE
- IDENTIFY THE JOB POSITION
- HIGHLIGHT YOUR STRENGTHS
- FOLLOW UP

LEGAL PLACEMENT AGENCY

"COVER LETTERS ARE THE FIRST VIEW OF AN APPLICANT. IT HAS TO BE A GREAT EXAMPLE OF WRITING. SPEND TIME THINKING ABOUT HOW BEST TO PORTRAY YOUR PROFESSIONAL IMAGE. WHAT ARE THE TWO MOST IMPORTANT ASSETS THAT YOU HAVE TO OFFER AN EMPLOYER? ANSWER THIS QUESTION IN YOUR COVER LETTER."

Once you complete your resume, you need to start on the cover letter. The cover letter is a two- or three-paragraph introduction to your resume that explains to the employer why you are applying for a particular position. As far as possible, the cover letter should be personalized and directed to a specific employer, rather than a generic "To Whom It May Concern." A cover letter is simple to prepare using the steps listed below.

Many people write a meaningless cover letter that states the obvious—"Enclosed please find my resume"—because they believe that employers do not read cover letters. However, most employers either look at the cover letter before reviewing the resume or, if they look at the resume first and it sparks their interest, go back and read the cover letter. With this in mind, consider that your cover letter will be either the opening statement or the closing argument of your application.

Follow the simple steps below to prepare a cover letter that will grab an employer's attention, and keep it, while he or she reads through your resume.

① READY: Five Easy Steps to a Fantastic Cover Letter

Your cover letter should be short and simple; it should contain no more than two or three paragraphs. As a general rule, the longer the cover letter, the less likely the employer is to read it thoroughly.

The format for a cover letter is the same whether you send it by mail, fax, or e-mail.

Step One: Format Your Cover Letter for Maximum Impact

Your cover letter should be prepared in the same format as a formal letter: with a date, the recipient's address, and a subject line:

April 15, 2006

Ms. Selia Ward
Cohens & Wood, L.L.P.
657 Main Street
Nowhere, State 89052

Re: Paralegal Position

Dear Ms. Ward,

If you do not know the name of the person in charge of hiring for the position, call the law office and ask. What might you say? "I am forwarding my application for the paralegal position to your firm. To whom should I address it?" Do not be put off by this direct approach; most firms will be impressed that you are taking the initiative. If the receptionist asks your name, give it and then ask how you can schedule an interview. This is a chance to make a connection with the receptionist; be extremely polite and thank him or her for the information.

If the receptionist will not give you the hiring manager's name, do not worry; simply address the letter to "Dear Hiring Manager" or "Dear Sir or Madam." Since the hiring manager's name is not being given out, everyone else will be using the same salutation, so this will not detract from your cover letter.

Make sure your cover letter provides your name, address, phone number, and e-mail address. If this information is not provided at the top or bottom of the letter, as with standard letterhead, include this contact information in your signature block. This is especially important in the event your cover letter becomes separated from your resume.

Jane Sullivan
678 Highland Drive
Nowhere, State 89078
890.555.9098
JaneSullivan@yahoo.com

Step Two: Tell the Reader You Are Applying for a Paralegal Position

The first paragraph of your cover letter should tell the reader (1) that you are applying for a paralegal position and (2) where you heard about the opening. This introductory paragraph is particularly important if you were referred by someone whose name rings a bell with the hiring manager. Make sure that you also send a follow-up letter of thanks to the individual who referred you to the position.

If you are responding to an advertisement, your first sentence might read: "In response to your advertisement for a paralegal in the *Saturday Review Journal,* I am enclosing my resume for your consideration." Be

> ### Example
> My instructor at Duke University, Moe Hardy, suggested I contact your office regarding the paralegal position in the litigation department.

clear and direct in your first paragraph: "Your advertisement for an experienced paralegal prompted me to contact you." Do not be overly confident or cocky: "You will find that I will be the best thing that ever happened to your firm"; will turn an employer off. You want to come across as professional and likeable—as a person who would fit in well with the law office culture.

Step Three: Highlight Your Qualifications

Highlight your qualifications for the position and tell the reader why you are a good candidate. Your resume sets forth your work history, so you do not need to present it again in your cover letter. Instead, identify the skills and qualifications that the employer is looking for (these should be listed in the advertisement) and indicate how your skills relate to the job requirements.

> ### Example
> I have experience with client and witness interviewing, field investigation, arbitration procedures, and legal research. I have prepared pleadings, discovery, motions, and legal memoranda. In addition, I am proficient in Windows, Word, Excel, PowerPoint, Lotus, WESTAW, and Lexis-Nexis. While working as a paralegal at the law firm of Jacobs & Marley, I received the award for Employee of the Month.

When it comes to your cover letter, remember some simple "don't"s. Do not sound desperate, as in "I really need to find a job to support myself and my four children." Do not send personal photos; law firms consider this inappropriate. Do not list your weaknesses, as in "I know that I do not have any experience in the legal profession." Do not lie—no example needed. Your cover letter is your sales pitch; you can explain your limited warranties later.

Your cover letter should be short, so identify significant accomplishments or awards you may have received, either as a paralegal or in a previous profession. For example, "During my 10 years as an elementary school teacher, I received the Teacher of the Year Award for the Clark County School District." Such professional acknowledgments indicate that you will be a dedicated and motivated employee for this law firm.

Step Four: Close with Consideration and Commitment

Your closing paragraph should (1) be complimentary and appreciative and (2) ask the employer for the opportunity to discuss your qualifications in person.

> ### Example
> Thank you for your time and consideration in reviewing my application. I look forward to meeting with you to discuss my qualifications.

Step Five: Sign Your Cover Letter and PROOFREAD

Do not forget to sign your cover letter. Of course you know that you need to sign your cover letter, but you would be surprised at how many applicants print out their cover letter and send it without signing it. After you print out your cover letter, sign it and proofread it more than once.

Most computer word-processing programs have spelling and grammar checks. This means that there really is no excuse for having basic spelling errors in your cover letter or your resume. Your cover letter is only a few short paragraphs, so read it and ask someone you know to read it. Do not try to make last-minute corrections such as adding a period with your black pen; reprint your resume, even if it delays you by a day. An error in the cover letter will typically mean that your resume will never be read.

⑪ SET: E-mail Cover Letters

Employers are increasingly soliciting applications via e-mail. E-mail cover letters tend to be shorter than a formal cover letter, in large part because the computer screen is smaller and the employer may quickly skim the cover letter before looking at the resume. However, e-mail cover letters require the same attention to detail as hard-copy letters.

Use proper capitalization, punctuation, and grammar when you write an e-mail cover letter, just as you would with any formal letter. It is common for e-mail writers to use all lowercase letters and omit punctuation; this is bad form and is not commonly accepted in law offices. In addition, you should always run a spell check before sending your e-mail; this will help you to catch errors you might otherwise overlook. Remember that spelling and grammar checks will not catch every error, so review each letter carefully before you hit "send." In fact, it is best to wait to address your e-mail until you are finished writing and reviewing the letter. This avoids accidentally hitting "send" on an incomplete letter or one that has not been proofread.

When formatting your e-mail cover letter, do not assume that bold, italics, or emoticons (symbols such as sideways happy faces :)) will be seen by the recipient; not all e-mail programs preserve text formatting, and emoticons are unprofessional. Once you send your e-mail letter, it is a good idea to follow it up with a hard copy sent via regular postal service "snail" mail. This ensures that your cover letter and resume will be seen by the firm, rather than possibly deleted at the click of a button by someone quickly reviewing the hundreds of e-mails in their inbox.

⊙ GO: A Final Note about Cover Letters

Remember that your cover letter makes your first impression on an employer. So draft your cover letter with the basics in mind: personalize your letter, keep in short (two or three paragraphs), highlight your qualifications, and *proofread*. A single error may take you out of the running.

⊙ Points to Consider

1. *Create a Draft Cover Letter.* Review job listings in your local newspaper. Draft a cover letter on the basis of the hiring criteria listed. Quickly draft a few paragraphs for your cover letter in the following format:

   Paragraph 1: List the position and how you heard about it.

   Paragraph 2: Highlight your qualifications.

   Paragraph 3: Close with a request for further discussion.

   Final paragraph: Sign and proofread.
2. *Contact Referrals.* If someone referred you to a position, send a note thanking him or her for the referral and confirming that you have followed up by contacting the firm.
3. *Proofread.* Make sure you proofread your cover letter and run spelling and grammar checks.

⊙ Job Search Tips

1. *Research.* Research job opportunities to determine employers' hiring criteria. Spell out how your qualifications address these criteria in your cover letter.
2. *Consider Network Referrals.* Take the opportunity to attend professional functions, such as paralegal/bar association and other community events. When you speak to people in the legal community, ask for their business cards. If someone suggests that you contact a particular attorney or firm,

immediately write down the firm's name as well as the name of the person who referred you. Compile this listing to review when you begin applying for positions.

Referral #1:
Name of firm/attorney referred to:
Address of firm/attorney:
Phone number of firm:
Referred by:

Referral #2:
Name of firm/attorney referred to:
Address of firm/attorney:
Phone number of firm:
Referred by:

CHAPTER 7

MAKING A GOOD FIRST IMPRESSION
Cover Letter Samples

The first impression is lasting, so make sure that your cover letter is professional. Review the cover letters and the commentaries included in this chapter to help you in creating your own cover letter.

COVER LETTERS

- PERSONALIZE YOUR COVER LETTER
- INDICATE THE POSITION YOU ARE APPLYING FOR
- HIGHLIGHT YOUR QUALIFICATIONS
- SIGN AND PROOFREAD

The purpose of a cover letter is to spark an employer's interest in you as an applicant. For that reason, your cover letter has to be more than a boring letter that announces that your resume is enclosed or simply rehashes your education and your work experience. A cover letter is a five-second advertisement and has to grab the employer's attention. Ideally, you should write a cover letter that impresses an employer enough to say, "Wow, I'd really like to talk to this person."

① READY: Find a Sample You Like

This chapter offers several cover letters with critical commentary to help you in creating your own cover letter. If you find a format that you like, adopt it in drafting your own cover letter. Every cover letter is unique, because each applicant has her or his own strengths and weaknesses, so do not worry that you are "copying" someone else's idea. This book is intended to give you ideas to help you create your own portfolio, so feel free to use any of the material.

⑪ SET: Key Points to Remember

In reviewing the sample cover letters and in drafting your own, keep in mind that a cover letter should
- be personalized.
- indicate the position you are applying for.
- highlight your specific qualifications for the position.
- state that you will follow up your contact, if you intend to do so.
- be signed and proofread.
- be short.

Personalize

Personalize your cover letter by naming the firm you are applying to, addressing the letter to the person doing the hiring, or, most effectively, mentioning the name of a person who referred you for the position (e.g., "Dean Flint recommended that I contact you regarding your paralegal position."); this name may ring a bell with your reader. Do not use "Mrs." or "Miss" in your salutation; instead, open the letter with "Ms." or "Mr."

Position

Indicate the position you are applying for. Some firms have several departments, and each department may conduct its own hiring, so be specific.

Highlight

Highlight your specific qualifications for the job without replaying your resume. Indicate your strengths (e.g., a hairdresser might note, "My extensive customer relations experience makes me uniquely qualified to provide client support for your firm."). Even if you do not think you fit the employer's qualifications, review your work history and consider how your experience will benefit this employer.

Follow Up

Indicate how you will follow up your initial contact, if you intend to do so. Although this is optional, many applicants find that it helps them to stand apart from the crowd; in addition, it does not hurt to have your name appear in front of the employer a second time. Mention to the reader that you will contact him or her later with a letter (if you do not have a phone number) or a phone call. This may motivate the reader to take some action on your resume.

Sign and Proofread

Sign and proofread your cover letter, or your resume may never be considered. Employers often receive cover letters that are unsigned; this shows them that the cover letter was not thoroughly proofread. Proofread your cover letter before you print it out, and read the hard copy as well. Errors are often overlooked on the computer screen, but you may be able to identify those mistakes on the hard copy.

Length

Keep your cover letter short. Cover letters should generally be no more than two or three paragraphs. A cover letter template is provided in Figure 7.1. This format shows the relevant sections usually expected in a cover letter.

FIGURE 7.1

Date

Your Name
Your Street Address
Your City, State   Zip

Hiring Manager's Name
Employer's Firm Name
Employer's Street Address/Post Office Box
Employer's City, State Zip

   re: Title of Position

Dear Ms. or Mr. (Name of Hiring Manager),

Paragraph 1: Identify the position to which you are applying and mention where the position was advertised.

Paragraph 2: Provide two to three brief paragraphs regarding your qualifications for the position.

Paragraph 3: Note that you look forward to hearing from the employer and to discussing your qualifications.

Sincerely,

Your Name

Enclosure: Resume

▶ GO: Start Writing

These five easy steps will help you draft an effective cover letter. Follow the outline provided in Figure 7.1 when you begin your own cover letter.

FIGURE 7.2

This is a dynamic cover letter that introduces the applicant with confidence

Good to list the position for reference

Find out. Is it Mr. or Ms.?

State purpose of writing

Watch line spacing

LESLIE MIROR
5810 Wispy Winds Street
Davis,California 95616

530.555.7474
530.555.9632
mandymiror@yahoo.com

February 9, 2007

A.Maron
Human Resources Department – Cirque Du Soleil
980 Main Street, Suite 200
Davis, California 95616

Re: Administrative Assistant

Dear A. Maron:

I am a highly experienced go-getter with a great attitude and a creative thinker who fits well in environments with diverse personalities. I'm very versatile, eager to learn and have the solid experience necessary for the responsibilities the position entails.

My computer skills are exceptional, being trained in Microsoft Office programs (i.e., Word, Excel and PowerPoint) and I type 70 words per minute. I am comfortable with the use of Dictaphone and transcription machines. I bring over five years experience, strong leadership competencies, firm judgment and decision-making abilities. I have trained new hires as well as temporary employees in office policies and procedures, taken on the role of office manager and have resolved conflict in a quick and efficient manner. I have created, edited and proofed legal pleadings, general correspondence, etc. I have performed research, file and supply management, prepared travel expense reports, made travel arrangements and various other administrative tasks.

I look forward to meeting with you so that we may further discuss my qualifications. I can be reached at any time with the telephone numbers listed above.

Thank you for your time and consideration.

Very truly yours,

Leslie S. Miror

FIGURE 7.3

LESLIE MIROR   530.555.7474
5810 Wispy Winds Street   530.555.9632
Davis, California 95616   mandymiror@yahoo.com

February 9, 2007

Ms. Andrea Maron
Human Resources Department – Cirque Du Soleil
980 Main Street, Suite 200
Davis, California 95616

>   *Re: Administrative Assistant*

Dear Ms. Maron:

I am writing to apply for the position of Administrative Assistant with Cirque Du Soleil. I am a highly experienced go-getter with a great attitude and a creative thinker who fits well in environments with diverse personalities. I'm very versatile, eager to learn and have the solid experience necessary for the responsibilities the position entails.

My computer skills are exceptional. I am trained in Microsoft Office programs including Word, Excel and PowerPoint and I type70 words per minute. I am comfortable with the use of a Dictaphone and transcription machines. I bring over five years experience, strong leadership competencies, firm judgment and decision-making abilities. I have also trained new-hires as well as temporary employees in office policies and procedures, taken on the role of office manager and have resolved conflict in a quick and efficient manner. I have created, edited and proofed legal pleadings, general correspondence, and other legal documents. I have performed research, file and supply management, prepared travel expense reports, made travel arrangements and various other administrative tasks.

I look forward to meeting with you so that we may further discuss my qualifications. I can be reached at any time at the telephone numbers listed above.

Thank you for your time and consideration.

Very truly yours,

Leslie S. Miror

Enclosure: Resume

FIGURE 7.4

Brandy K.Lige
564 Shale Circle
Henderson, NV 89052
702.555.9848
brandy@accesscom.com

Insert addressee's address

14 June 2007

This cover letter has three major problems:
1. the change of font size indicates it was not proofread thoroughly
2. it does not tell the reader about the applicant's skills, because the wording is vague
3. it does not highlight the candidate's strengths ("ample experience" is very weak)

Dear Ms. Powers:

I am responding to your ad in the *Las Vegas Review Journal* for a Docket Clerk. I am interested in eventually becoming a paralegal for your firm.

Before earning my paralegal certificate, I worked primarily in the field of education. My prior experiences highlighted and strengthened skills that characterize a good legal professional. I am highly organized and detail-oriented. My verbal and written communication skills are effective, and I have ample experience working under pressure.

This is an obvious statement and should not be included; clearly your contact information will be used to contact you

I look forward to hearing from you. Please contact me using the information provided at the top of this letter. Thank you for your consideration.

Leave room for your signature!

Sincerely,
Brandy K. Lige

This person is an experienced elementary school teacher and should introduce her management and organizational skills, interpersonal abilities, plan development experience, and more in this cover letter

Enclosure: resume

FIGURE 7.5

Brandy K. Lige
555 Shale Circle
Henderson, NV 89052
702.555.9848
brandy@accesscom.com

June 14, 2007

Ms. Melanie Powers
244 Tropicana Avenue
Las Vegas, Nevada 89059

Re: Docket Clerk

Dear Ms. Powers:

I am responding to your ad in the *Las Vegas Review Journal* for a Docket Clerk. I am entering the paralegal profession and would like to obtain experience with scheduling and project management.

Before earning my paralegal certificate at the University of California, Berkeley, I worked as an elementary school teacher for twelve years. I received the Alameda County District Teacher of the Year Award in 2003 and again in 2005. I effectively planned and managed core curriculum for more than twenty-five third grade students during each academic year.

I am highly organized and detail-oriented. I am familiar with all forms of legal document preparation, including drafting complaints, summons, discovery documents and motions.

I look forward to an opportunity to discuss my qualifications for this position. Thank you for your consideration.

Sincerely,

Brandy K. Lige

Enclosure: resume

FIGURE 7.6

This is an example of a cover letter that just reviews the candidate's resume. A cover letter should add to the resume

Addressee's address

The applicant should highlight specific qualifications and accomplishments

Watch word spacing

Jason L. Cortez

1082 Sigrid Drive
Durham, North Carolina 27708
Day: 919-555-3192
Evening: 919-684-3192 or 919-555-9688
Jason@hotmail.com

Dear Sir/Madam:

I am applying for the position your company recently posted as being available. I am enclosing my resume for your review.

I hold an Associates of Art Degree in Political Science from the Community College of North Carolina and a Paralegal Certificate from Duke University. I have experience in legal research and document preparation, including pleadings, discovery, and motions. Please refer to my enclosed resume, which further substantiates my qualifications, education, and experience.

I would appreciate the opportunity to discuss my qualifications with you. I am experienced in customer relations and recognize how important and essential your clients are to your business.

For the past four years, I have been learning about working in the legal field and I look forward to the new challenges that I will face as aparalegal. I am confident that I can accomplish any task presented to me while being on-time and within budget.

My multiple skills and knowledge make me a strong candidate for this position. I hope to have the opportunity to discuss this position with you personally.

Thank you for your consideration.
Respectfully yours,

Jason L. Cortez
919-684-3182
Jason@hotmail.com
Enclosure: Resume

FIGURE 7.7

Jason L. Cortez

1082 Sigrid Drive
Durham, North Carolina 27708
Day: 919-555-3192
Evening: 919-684-3192 or 919-555-9688
Jason@hotmail.com

Speilbery, Crony and Wine
3259 Sir Arthur Lane
Durham, North Carolina 27708

Re: Paralegal Position

Dear Hiring Manager:

I am applying for the paralegal position your company recently posted at Duke University. I offer excellent interpersonal communication skills and document preparation experience.

I hold an Associates of Art Degree in Political Science and a Paralegal Certificate from Duke University. I have experience in legal research, document preparation, including pleadings, practice, and motions. In addition to my paralegal education, I have worked in the food service industry for several years. This experience has helped me to develop excellent interpersonal communication and organizational skills which will be an asset to my future employer. I am a creative thinker and I learn quickly.

The multiple skills and knowledge that I posses make me a strong candidate for this position. I hope to have the opportunity to discuss this position with you personally. Thank you for your consideration.

Respectfully yours,

Jason Cortez

Enclosure: Resume

FIGURE 7.8

January 27, 2007

Cooksey, Toolen, Gage, Duffy, & Woog
Attn.: Griff Hayden

RE: Paralegal Position

Mr. Hayden:

Enclosed please find my resume for your review and consideration for the Paralegal position that your firm has available. I believe my experience and education make me an ideal candidate for this position.

I have recently moved to the Boulder area to be near family and am currently enrolled in the Paralegal Certificate Program at the University of Colorado. I have a Bachelor of Science degree in Criminal Justice. I am flexible and have a desire to enter a new career path.

With over 10 years of analytical and technical work, I am organized, efficient, detail oriented, and conscientious. I have excellent verbal and written communication skills and am computer literate. I am a quick learner and able to work independently and in a team environment. My background also includes extensive experience in reasearching, interpreting and applying State and Federal laws, rules, and regulations.

I am interested in meeting with you to discuss my qualifications in an interview at your convenience. My telephone number is 704.555.9878.

Thank you for your time and consideration.

Sincerely,

Lisa D. Lawless
50 Boulder Falls
Charlotte, North Carolina 28223
704.555.9878

This cover letter is very good; it describes in detail her experience in the third paragraph, including her legal experience

Oop, watch spelling errors

Do not put phone number in the body of the letter when you provide it for reference

Full name and address should be provided

FIGURE 7.9

January 27, 2007

Cooksey, Toolen, Gage, Duffy, & Woog, LLC
Attn.: Griff Hayden
4375 First Avenue
Boulder, CO 80302

RE: Paralegal Position

Dear Mr. Hayden:

Enclosed please find my resume for your review and consideration for the Paralegal position that your firm has available. I believe my experience and education make me an ideal candidate for this position.

I have recently moved to the Boulder area to be near family and am currently enrolled in the Paralegal Certificate Program at the University of Colorado. I have a Bachelor of Science degree in Criminal Justice. I am flexible and have a desire to enter a new career path.

With over 10 years of analytical and technical work, I am organized, efficient, detail oriented, and conscientious. I have excellent verbal and written communication skills and am computer literate. I am a quick learner and able to work independently and in a team environment. My background also includes extensive experience in researching, interpreting and applying State and Federal laws, rules, and regulations.

I am interested in meeting with you to discuss my qualifications in an interview at your convenience. Thank you for your time and consideration.

Sincerely,

Lisa D. Lawless
50 Boulder Falls
Charlotte, North Carolina 28223
704.555.9878

Enclosure: Resume

FIGURE 7.10

Everything is wrong with this letter: 1. it should be properly addressed
2. it should provide contact information
3. it should highlight the applicant's strengths

Note whether a resume is enclosed

June 29, 2007

Dear Mr. Kale,

I am very interested in the Paralegal postion with your company. I am a professional, responsible person who is dedicated to bringing the utmost quality and efficiency to whichever position I hold.

I am proficient in Outlook Express, Word, Excel, PowerPoint, as well as other programs. I also have experience with Lexis-Nexis.

Please call me at any time to discuss setting an appointment for an interview.

Sincerely,

Shaleema Obama

FIGURE 7.11

Shaleema Obama

728 Garnet Court   *(406) 555-4345*
Missoula, Montana 59801

ShaleemaObama@msn.com

May 29, 2007

Justine Kale
Jusper, Mickelson, & Wooley
679 Main Street
Summerlin, Nevada 89067

    Re: Paralegal Position

Dear Mr. Kale,

I am very interested in the Paralegal postion with your company. I am a professional, responsible person who is dedicated to bringing the utmost quality and efficiency to my work.

I am proficient in Outlook Express, Word, Excel, PowerPoint, as well as Lexis-Nexis. I am experienced in legal document preparation as well as legal research. I am re-locating and seeking a new position in the Las Vegas area.

Please call me at any time to discuss setting an appointment for an interview.

I look forward to hearing from you.

Sincerely,

Shaleema Obama
728 Garnet Court
Missoula, Montana 59801
(406) 555-4345
ShaleemaObama@msn.com

Enclosure: Resume

FIGURE 7.12

Yikes!!
This candidate is incredibly well qualified but you cannot tell it from this cover letter. English is this student's second language and the letter should be proofread by a native speaker. The salutation is too informal; the letter should be addressed to Ms. Williams — always be formal

Don't use abbreviations in cover letters

Helen Williams
Staffing Office
501 S. Rancho Drive, Ste G-46
El Cerrito, California 94530

Re: Paralegal Position

Dear Helen:

I am finished with my paralegal courses at UCD and ready for work. As you did not receive the attached copy of my résumé via e-mail, I am responding to your request and attaching it herewith for your consideration.

If you wish to contact me, I can be reached during the day at (530) 435-0740.

Sincerely yours,

Jamal Spender

Attachment: resume

FIGURE 7.13

Helen Williams
Staffing Office
501 S. Rancho Drive, Ste G-46
El Cerito, California 94530
(530) 555-0740

　　　Re: Paralegal Position

Dear Ms. Williams:

I am writing regarding the Paralegal position you advertised in the *California Lawyer*. I recently completed my paralegal courses at the University of California, Davis and am interested in working with your firm.

I have experience with legal terminology, court structure, and legal procedures. In addition, I have experience preparing discovery documents and motions.

I look forward to having the opportunity to discussing my qualifications with you.

Sincerely yours,

Jamal Spender

Attachment: resume

Jamal Spender
560 Eighth Street
Sacramento, California   89056
(910) 555-9087
JSpenderUCDParalegal@yahoo.com

FIGURE 7.14

This cover letter is a good example and clearly tells the reader that the applicant is highly recommended

January 11, 2008

Keith Anderson
Bruce & Davis
789 Main Street
Davis, California 95616

Re: Paralegal Position

Dear Mr. Anderson,

I am responding to your advertisement in the University of California, Davis Bulletin for paralegal to assist you. My work with first-rate attorneys enables me to offer you an exceptional mix of training, knowledge, experience, and professionalism.

As you will see on the enclosed résumé, I have worked for several law firms in the Sacramento area. I am proficient in many areas of general civil litigation, bankruptcy, business transactions, and civil trials. As a result, I can offer you an unusual level of expertise in researching complaints and discovery requests as well as responses to counterclaims, motions for discovery sanctions, motions for summary judgments, and motions to dismiss.

The attorney with whom I work is retiring and therefore I am looking for a new position. He has provided me with superior recommendations to aid me in my search. I would appreciate the opportunity to present this recommendation to you, and to introduce myself as a candidate for the position at your firm.

If you will contact me at (530) 555-0740 during the day or evening, we can schedule an appointment.

Sincerely,

Jake Ewing

Attachment: Resume

● Points to Consider

1. Identify Your Qualifications. Identify three skills or outstanding achievements to highlight in your cover letter.
   Skill/achievement #1:

   Skill/achievement #2:

   Skill/achievement #3:

2. Cover Letter Format. Choose a format that appeals to you from the sample cover letters. Note the common drafting mistakes made by the writers. Confirm that your cover letter is free of these errors.

● Job Search Tips

1. Obtain Contact Information. Contact firms that have listings for paralegal positions in your area. Find out the names of the respective hiring managers for inclusion in your cover letters.
2. E-mail Cover Letter. Prepare an e-mail cover letter for electronic submission by removing the formatting from your cover letter draft.

CHAPTER 8

JOB SEARCH TECHNIQUES
Where to Start

Beginning your job search is like searching for the prize in the cereal box: there is a lot of cereal to dig through before you find the treasure.

JOB SEARCH

- SCHOOL JOB BOARD POSTINGS
- CAREER FAIRS
- NEWSPAPER ADVERTISEMENTS
- PARALEGAL/BAR ASSOCIATION ADVERTISEMENTS
- GOVERNMENT LISTINGS
- EMPLOYMENT SERVICES
- INTERNET SEARCHES
- COLD CALLING/ MARTINDALE-HUBBELL
- NETWORKING

The paralegal profession is one of the fastest-growing professions across the country. The legal profession is increasingly becoming aware that paralegals are an important resource for attorneys, government agencies, and small business owners. In addition, many paralegals find that freelancing offers them greater flexibility in managing their careers. Consider all of your options during your job search.

Finding the right job requires hard work, patience, and plenty of time. You need to identify the practice area you are interested in (e.g., family law, construction defect, business), the type of environment you want to work in (large or small firm), and what type of firm culture you are looking for (formal, low-key, casual), in addition to practical considerations such as the hours required, flexibility for family schedules, the firm's distance from your home, and your salary requirements. The paralegal job market is competitive, so be prepared to stand out from the other applicants as you begin your job search.

If you are just beginning your career in the legal profession, it is helpful to view your first paralegal job as a "training ground," an opportunity for you to gain experience in a law office environment. Employers recognize this and generally expect to dedicate a portion of their time to training you. This may affect the compensation package; training a paralegal uses the firm's time and resources, and therefore your initial salary and job choices may reflect this. Consider these issues when you research the available job opportunities.

① READY: Choosing a Practice Area

Before you begin applying for positions, consider the area of law that you would like to enter. Paralegal employment opportunities are available in family law, personal injury, construction, bankruptcy, business law, immigration, real estate, estate planning, criminal law, and gov-

HIRING MANAGER

"PRACTICALLY SPEAKING, AN INDIVIDUAL WHO IS NEW TO THE PARALEGAL PROFESSION MAY NEED TO CONSIDER ACCEPTING AN ENTRY-LEVEL POSITION IN ORDER TO GAIN SOME EXPERIENCE IN THE FIELD. OUR FIRM OFTEN HIRES RECENT GRADUATES AT ENTRY-LEVEL SALARIES IN ORDER TO ASSESS THEIR ABILITY TO PERFORM PARALEGAL WORK. AFTER SIX MONTHS, IF THE NEW HIRE PROVES HIMSELF, WE WILL PROMOTE HIM AND INCREASE HIS SALARY BASE. ALL FIRMS HAVE SIMILAR EVALUATION PERIODS, ALTHOUGH THEY MAY NOT IDENTIFY THIS TO NEW EMPLOYEES."

ernmental agencies, as well as non-traditional arenas. In some areas, particularly rural environments where opportunities are limited, you may not have the luxury of choosing a practice area; you may simply be applying for *any* available job opportunities. Research your options before you begin your job search; this will help to guide you in the application process.

Internships

A great way to determine whether you are interested in a particular area of law is through an internship. Several schools offer internship programs for their students for just this purpose. However, you can create your own internship if you have the time and initiative to make a few phone calls.

Many law firms need someone to complete mundane tasks, such as filing, data entry, answering phones, running errands, or scheduling, and others offer legal research opportunities, shepardizing duties, or document preparation. Whatever the job, do not underestimate the value of having experience, of any kind, in a law office. Working in a law office will offer you an inside perspective into the duties and responsibilities of a paralegal—even if you are not performing paralegal services. Just being in the firm allows you to talk, watch, listen, and learn. In addition, you will have the opportunity to ask questions of the paralegals, attorneys, and other staff members to help you familiarize yourself with the legal profession.

Although some internships are paid, most are volunteer positions. Therefore, law firms often welcome the opportunity to have a volunteer intern in their office for a period of time. Even if you are not part of an organized internship program, create your own opportunity by getting on the phone and offering your services to law firms in the area. You may begin work as a volunteer, but if the firm is impressed with your professionalism and work performance it may hire you for a paid position. So create your own destiny by taking a walk through the yellow pages or through other legal listings, such as Martindale-Hubbell.

Hiring Criteria

Advertisements for job positions are full of information about the employer's hiring criteria, including work experience, computer skills, typing specifications, and educational requirements. This information will help you in tailoring your cover letter and your resume to the needs of a particular employer.

What if you do not meet the employer's hiring criteria? When you are beginning your job search, you may find it discouraging that many job listings indicate that the employer requires years of experience in the legal profession or in a specific legal field. An employer may also require specific computer skills and typing speed. If you do not meet these requirements, should you apply for the job anyway? Yes!

Employers may have preconceptions of the qualifications required for new employees. However, a surprising number of employers hire people who do not have all of the qualifications listed in the job advertisement. Why? Because employers are looking for someone who is a "good fit" for the office, that is, someone whom the hiring manager likes and believes will get along well with others in the firm.

Obviously, this does not mean that your qualifications are not important, because they are. However, if an employer has offered you an interview after reviewing your resume, this indicates that your qualifications are sufficient for the position. Therefore, if a job sounds interesting, pursue it; something on your resume may spark the employer's interest in extending an interview to you.

Martindale-Hubbell: A Guidebook to Law Firms

Martindale-Hubbell should be a job hunter's best friend. This multivolume "encyclopedia" of law firms is invaluable in providing information about a law firm and the attorneys practicing with the firm. If you are responding to an advertised position or following up on a referral, it is helpful to go to Martindale-Hubbell to learn about the firm's practice areas and view professional biographical information about the firm's associates and partners (including schools attended, membership in professional associations, articles authored, and major cases argued).

Martindale-Hubbell is available at all major law libraries, as well as on-line at http://www.martindale.com. The hardbound volumes of Martindale-Hubbell are generally to be found in the reference section of your law library. They are yellow, with black or red spines. They are published periodically and are accessed alphabetically by state (listed on the spine), by city (listed on the top of each page), and then by firm name within each city. Each listing provides information about the firm's area of practice as well as biographical information on the firm's associates and partners, including schools attended, membership in professional associations, articles authored, and major cases. These can be important pieces of information to help you prepare for the interview.

Martindale-Hubbell's on-line site provides the same information free of charge to the user. This site is user friendly and allows you to search the name of an attorney or a law firm, a practice area (e.g., family law, bankruptcy, immigration), or geographical area. If you are just beginning your job search, this is an excellent resource to consider. Type in your geographical location and a practice area that interests you; this will provide an initial list of firms to consider in your job search.

Martindale-Hubbell should be a job hunter's best friend, but remember that not all law firms or law offices are listed, because it is a paid subscription service. In addition, government agencies are not included, nor are community outreach programs. However, a significant number of firms are included each year and it is a valuable resource for job hunters. Many job seekers also use Martindale-Hubbell to do cold calling and mailings, a technique discussed below.

(II) SET: Where to Begin

Your job search can and should include several avenues:

- school job board postings
- career fairs
- newspaper advertisements
- paralegal association advertisements
- bar association advertisements, including bar journals
- government listings
- employment services
- Internet searches
- cold calling/Martindale-Hubbell
- networking

School Job Board Postings

School job board postings are targeted specifically to graduates of your program, generally because your program has gained a reputation for providing qualified and skilled paralegals. It is best to begin your job search at the job board located at your college or university. Many universities post job opportunities on their student Web site; with a click of your mouse, you may be able to find a position and send your resume to the employer on-line.

Job board postings are created when employers contact your program director looking for graduates to fill their paralegal positions. These employers want to hire graduates of your program, and they generally expect to hire recent graduates, so these postings should be looked at first.

Most job board postings tell you the name of the firm advertising a position. This is a great benefit in preparing your resume and cover letter and tailoring it to the practice area and needs of the firm. Refer to Martindale-Hubbell or conduct an on-line search to learn about the firm and its attorneys. If no information is available, ask other paralegals, attorneys, or your instructors what they know about the firm. Their knowledge may be valuable in helping you to prepare your cover letter.

Career Fairs

Career fairs are hosted by local schools, universities, and chambers of commerce to offer students and other applicants exposure to a large group of employers. These events are an excellent way to learn about opportunities in both the private and public sectors. Although many career fairs do not specifically cater to the legal profession, employers may be hiring for opportunities in their legal department, so do not miss out. In addition, career fairs allow applicants to meet and greet recruiters and other hiring personnel—and to make a positive first impression. If you are interested in making initial contact with several employers in a short period, this is the place to be. Companies often have several positions they are hiring for, and you just might fit the bill for one of the jobs.

Keep in mind that career fairs are structured for both you and the employer to meet and greet. These venues offer employers the opportunity to meet prospective applicants quickly and efficiently and to get a quick look at the individual's personal presentation. Therefore, prepare by dressing professionally, carrying several copies of your resume, and putting your best foot forward. A two-minute exchange can lead to a great legal career.

Newspaper Advertisements

The classified listings from your local paper offer an excellent way to find job opportunities in your area. Most newspapers also list job openings on-line, and these listings are often easier to access than the daily paper. Although job classifieds often provide a long list of the employer's hiring criteria, they often give little, if any, information about the employer.

Legal positions advertised in the newspaper generally do not list the name of the law firm or a phone number to contact the firm. They often read simply, "Estate planning firm seeks paralegal . . . ." In addition, you may be applying via a Post Office Box or a general fax number when responding to a classified advertisement. This obviously makes it difficult to customize your cover letter and your resume. Nonetheless, send your resume with a cover letter, even if it is generic.

If the advertisement offers a phone number, call the number and find out the name of the firm, then do your research. If you are able to call the firm directly, tell the receptionist that you are applying for the advertised paralegal position and ask the name of the person who will be conducting the hiring; remember to double-check the spelling of the name before you hang up.

Keep in mind that an employment position is generally advertised *after* employers have exhausted all other avenues for finding a qualified paralegal. Therefore, the firm may be more flexible in its stated hiring criteria.

Paralegal and Bar Association Advertisements

Professional legal associations often provide job listings for paralegals and legal assistants. Many of these listings are available on-line or through the association's periodical publications. The most commonly recognized legal associations that provide listings include

- the National Association of Legal Assistants (NALA)
- the National Federation of Paralegal Associations (NFPA)
- state bar associations
- local paralegal and bar associations

These resources often list job opportunities throughout the country and can be found through a quick on-line search using the organization's name. However, unless you are willing to relocate, you may find only a limited number of positions available in your area.

ATTORNEY

"OUR FIRM ALWAYS HAS A LAUNDRY LIST OF QUALIFICATIONS IN OUR JOB ADVERTISEMENTS. WE CALL IT OUR EMPLOYEE WISH LIST AND CONSIDER IT LIKE A CHILD'S CHRISTMAS LIST FOR SANTA. WE WOULD LOVE TO FIND AN APPLICANT WHO MEETS ALL OF OUR WISH LIST CRITERIA, BUT REALISTICALLY WE MAY GET ONLY A FEW OF THE THINGS WE WANTED. WE GENERALLY LIST THE QUALIFICATIONS OF OUR OUTGOING PARALEGAL BUT WE DON'T NECESSARILY EXPECT AN INCOMING PARALEGAL TO MEET EVERY ITEM LISTED."

Government Listings

Local, state, and federal governments employ thousands of paralegals across the United States as well as abroad. Most government agencies post job positions on their official Web sites or through local offices. In addition, many of these positions can be found through searchable databases such as http://www.publicservice.monster.com and http://www.paralegal-jobs.com. To find local job postings, start calling your city, county, and state agencies to determine how to locate their employment opportunities; most of them will have on-line listings that allow you to send your resume via e-mail.

The federal government also offers a variety of postings through official Web sites, such as http://www.usajobs.opm.gov and http://fedworld.gov. America's Job Bank, found at http://www.ajb.dni.us, also offers government listings and boasts more than 3,000 paralegal job opportunities. Other government employment opportunities can be searched through http://govspot.com and http://governmentjobs.com. Although government jobs may not pay as well as jobs in the private sector, they generally offer better health benefit packages, vacation and personal leave schedules, and job security. So check out what employment opportunities your government has to offer you.

Employment Services

Employment agencies can be an excellent resource for finding paralegal positions available in your area. The positions may be available temporarily or they may begin as full-time permanent positions. A common misconception is that employment agencies charge you, the employee, for making a placement. In fact, most employment placement firms do not charge the employee any out-of-pocket costs; they charge the employer if a placement is made.

Employment agencies can save you time and legwork in looking for a position. An employment agency screens your resume and conducts an initial interview with you. If you meet the employer's qualifications, the agency will then recommend you to the employer for an interview. Many firms like this selection process because it saves them time and money. However, agencies generally adhere strictly to the employer's hiring criteria (legal experience, computer skills, etc.), so if you do not meet these qualifications, you will not be referred for the position. There are, of course, exceptions, so if you can blow their socks off, you may still secure an interview with the employer.

Consider this alternative if you do not find a job in your expected timeframe.

Cold Calling

The average person thinks, "Yuck, I hate cold calling!" However, cold calling can be a goldmine. It is a great chance to find positions that have not been advertised. This approach allows you to tailor your job search to firms specializing in a practice area in which you are interested.

What's more, you can contact firms that are conveniently located to where you live, cutting down on your commute time. What could be better?

So how do you start? Using resources such as Martindale-Hubbell, bar directories, yellow pages, and law firm Web sites, locate firms in your area. Then read about their areas of practice and find out about the attorneys with whom you could be working.

Call the firm you are interested in and tell the receptionist, "I'm looking for a paralegal position in a [real estate, family law, estate planning, etc.] law firm. I read about your firm in Martindale-Hubbell and I would like to speak with your hiring manager." You could also bypass the receptionist by asking to speak with the hiring manager directly and then starting a dialogue about your job search.

If cold calling seems too overwhelming, many of the listings provide fax numbers as well as phone numbers, so if you just cannot bring yourself to make a call, fax a cover letter and resume, noting your interest in their practice area. If you happen to be in a position to drop off your resume to the firm, make sure that you dress professionally when you do so; every interaction you have with the firm will make an impression.

Of course, do not forget the classic yellow pages. Many firms are not listed in Martindale-Hubbell and do not maintain their own Web site—particularly small firms that may be conveniently located to your home. Look through the yellow pages, choose firms that you find interesting, and call them. Have some type of a script prepared of what you will say (e.g., "I am a paralegal interested in working in the local area"). Although cold calling may not be appealing to you, it may be a goldmine of opportunity just waiting to be tapped. Do not underestimate this alternative for finding employment.

Internet Searches

Today, you can locate job offerings with the click of your mouse. The Internet offers thousands of job opportunities in the legal sector, and a multitude of sites are available to job seekers. Use the key words "paralegal employment opportunities" or "paralegal jobs" in a search engine and you will discover hundreds of paralegal positions available in markets across the country. Chapter 9 provides specific guidance and listings for Internet job searches. Although the Web can be a valuable resource for job seekers in large metropolitan areas, it is generally not the most effective tool for those in rural areas.

Networking

Networking is a great way to find a job. Talk to classmates, attend meetings of your local paralegal association, talk to other paralegals and attorneys, attend political events, or discuss your job search with members of your church or other community organizations. The key is to get out of your "comfort zone" and start advertising yourself. Remember, employers generally hire people they know or learn about through

PARALEGAL

"THE BEST JOB I EVER HAD I FOUND FROM COLD CALLING. THE FIRM WAS SMALL AND LOCATED NEAR MY HOME. THEY KNEW THEY NEEDED TO HIRE A PARALEGAL BUT HADN'T YET TAKEN THE STEPS TO ADVERTISE. I CALLED THEM AND THE MANAGING PARTNER ASKED ME TO COME IN THAT WEEK. THEY HIRED ME ON THE SPOT AND I STARTED THE FOLLOWING DAY. I HAD NO COMPETITION FOR THE JOB BECAUSE I CREATED THE OPENING MYSELF."

others. So get to know people around you and put yourself in situations that provide opportunities to talk to others.

PARALEGAL
INSTRUCTOR

"ONE SEMESTER I HAD A
STUDENT WHO REFERRED
THREE OF HER CLASSMATES
TO HER LAW FIRM FOR
PARALEGAL POSITIONS; ALL
OF THEM WERE HIRED. THIS
WAS A WIN-WIN SITUATION.
THE STUDENTS DIDN'T HAVE
TO POUND THE PAVEMENT
LOOKING FOR JOBS AND THE
EMPLOYER HAD A GREAT
SOURCE FOR FINDING
TRAINED PARALEGALS."

▶ GO: Search and Ye Shall Find . . .

Begin your job search today, even if you simply peruse the newspaper's classified ads. Remember to look not only for positions for "Paralegals" and "Legal Assistants" but also for related job positions. It is important to "think out of the box." Paralegals can apply for job positions as law librarians, contract administrators, mediators, human resource specialists, legal editors, teachers, and more.

Do not get discouraged by rejection during this phase of your job search: everyone will experience it. In law school, we used to wallpaper our study areas with rejection letters while reminding ourselves of the words of our employment coordinator: "It takes only one." Remember, you need only *one* job.

◉ Points to Consider

1. *Identify Areas of Practice.* Identify three fields of practice you are interested in pursuing.
   Area #1:
   Area #2:
   Area #3:
2. *Create a Personal Job Bank.* Identify two job opportunities from each of the following resources:
   Newspaper advertisements
   Listing #1:
   Listing #2:
   Paralegal association advertisements
   Listing #1:
   Listing #2:
   Bar association advertisements, including bar journals
   Listing #1:
   Listing #2:
   Government listings
   Listing #1:
   Listing #2:
   Employment services
   Listing #1:
   Listing #2:
   Cold calling/Martindale-Hubbell
   Listing #1:
   Listing #2:
   Internet searches
   Listing #1:
   Listing #2:
   Networking
   Listing #1:
   Listing #2:

◉ Job Search Tips

1. *Research Government Positions.* Research employment positions with the state and federal governments through the following sites:
   - http://www.publicservice.monster.com
   - http://www.paralegal-jobs.com
   - http://www.usajobs.opm.gov
   - http://fedworld.gov
   - http://www.ajb.dni.us
   - http://govspot.com
   - http://governmentjobs.com

2. *Research Local Government Positions.* Local government agencies provide on-line listings for employment positions through various public agencies. Search with the keywords "paralegal jobs" or "legal assistant jobs" and the name of your local city or county to find these listings.

CHAPTER 9

GET WIRED
Finding On-line Job Opportunities

The Internet is an amazing resource for job seekers. It is a fast and efficient method to help you find a paralegal position.

ON-LINE SEARCH

- START CLICKING
- SEARCH "PARALEGAL JOBS"
- VISIT RELEVANT SITES
- FIND JOB LISTINGS
- POST YOUR RESUME
- CLICK AND SEND

The World Wide Web offers great opportunities for job seekers in large metropolitan areas, as well as others who are willing to relocate. In addition to the many large searchable databases, such as http://www.monster.com and http://www.paralegal-jobs.com, law firms, government agencies, bar associations, and legal periodicals commonly list job openings on their home pages. The key to a successful job search on the Web is to learn how to surf the Web effectively, and not get trapped in it.

One simple fact will help you to put your Internet job search in perspective: law firms do not have the time or resources to find you; you have to find them. Most law firms do not have full-time recruiters who can review the hundreds of resumes posted on Internet databases. Therefore, simply posting a resume is not likely to yield many results.

Approach your Internet job search as you would any employment listing: search, find, and conquer . . . that is, contact.

ⓘ READY: Electronic Resumes

Most employers want your resume as a fully formatted Word document or as a pdf file. However, as law firms often lag behind in their electronic capabilities, you may be asked to submit your resume as a text file (.txt). If the firm stores resumes as text files rather than graphics, your beautifully designed resume needs to be stripped down to a basic text file that can easily be e-mailed to an employer. Although few law firms maintain large databases of resumes that they search as jobs become available, many firms do streamline their hiring with electronic submissions.

When preparing an electronic submission, you should follow these guidelines:

- omit formatting
- use left margin alignment

- omit bolding, italicization, underlining
- omit shadow boxes
- use all capitals to emphasize material
- replace bullets with + or > or *
- replace lines with =
- use one font style
- do not use tab, line, or paragraph indents

Figure 9.1 shows how an electronic resume might look. Although this may seem like a boring presentation, it is best to submit your resume in this simple format to avoid errors and modifications that otherwise may occur in a formatted resume in transit to another system. If you are determined to retain your original formatting, you can send your resume as a pdf file.

Emailing Cover Letters

You will most likely be required to e-mail your cover letter at some point during your job search. Therefore, you need to be aware of a few common pitfalls many candidates fall into during this process.

Most employers hate mass e-mails, so it is best to customize your resume when sending it via e-mail. This does not mean that you should use the mail-merge function, which might result in your salutation reading "Dear <?xml:namespace prefix=o ns=urn:schemas-microsoft-com: office/>", obviously telling your readers that they have received a mass e-mail. Moreover, mass e-mails may be caught in an employer's spam filter, and you may find yourself blocked out from the employer's system. Maximize the effectiveness of your e-mails by customizing them as much as possible for each position.

In addition, be wise and avoid sending your e-mail from your work e-mail address. Most companies monitor their employees' e-mail accounts, and this probably will not play well with your employer. In addition, if you find yourself without a job, you will lose your address book as well as the e-mail address where a prospective employer will likely contact you back. Slight problem.

If you are sending an e-mail, make sure that you get the reader's attention with a well-drafted subject line. This ensures that your message will be opened and read. Consider a short and informative description of your e-mail, such as "Paralegal Position." If your subject line is too long, employers will not be able to view it unless they open your e-mail, so the e-mail is likely to get deleted. Be direct and list the position you are applying for. Do not get fancy with a subject line such as "Best Paralegal in the West." In addition, be wise in drafting your message and fill out the "To:" line *after* you have completed the perfect letter. Too often we accidentally click "Send" before we are done with the message. This mistake is understandable, but it is also unprofessional and should be considered when sending any e-mail out. As a final note, it is a good practice to follow an e-mail with a U.S. Mail hard copy of your resume, in the event the hiring manager has a backlog with her inbox.

FIGURE 9.1

RICHARD FLINT

4567 Muror Dr.
Gainsville, Florida 32611
(352) 555-4908 Home
(352) 555-0098 Cellular
richardflint@hotmail.com

OBJECTIVE
To obtain a paralegal position with a business law firm.

EDUCATION
UNIVERSITY OF MONTANA, Missoula, Montana
B.A., PARALEGAL STUDIES

* General course of paralegal studies
* Prepared legal documents, including pleadings, discovery, and motions
* Substantive coursework in Family Law, Contracts, Criminal Law, and Business Law

EXPERIENCE
2005-Present
PARALEGAL, Peel and Brimley/Gainsville, Florida

* Prepare discovery documents for construction defect firm
* Responsible for coordinating and scheduling firm depositions and trials
* Conduct legal research and trial preparation

2003-2005
MANAGER, Capital Works/Gainsville, Florida

* Customer service representative for 40 accounts
* Maintained customer invoicing and payroll accounts
* Supervised ten employees

2000-2003
AGENT, Travel Services/Las Vegas, Nevada

* Responsible for sales and marketing of travel services
* Scheduled customer travel arrangements
* Maintained office files

Fax Resumes

Many law firms ask applicants to fax their resume to the firm's office. You can generally fax your standard formatted resume, unless the employer directs otherwise. However, following a few simple guidelines will maximize the presentation of a faxed resume:

- print your resume on a laser printer
- use white 8½ × 11-inch paper
- use standard paper weight
- avoid underlining and shadowing
- list your name at the top of each page

Fax machines tend to change the appearance of your resume. Following these tips will help you to prepare a resume that can be faxed without substantial distortion.

⑪ SET: On-line Paralegal Job Listings

It is easy to get overwhelmed by all of the Web site options that are available to help you in your job search. The key is to find the sites that provide the most recent listings for your area. Choose a search engine and enter "paralegal or legal assistant jobs," or some variant, and you will find several employment-related sites. These sites are generally free to the job seeker; if you find one that is not, move down your list. Employment databases such as http://www.monster.com are supported by employers and recruiters, who pay to post job openings and to access the list of on-line resumes.

Take time to check out the listings that each site provides; you will see that some of the sites offer more job opportunities in certain geographical areas than others. There are hundreds of job site options, but the more helpful paralegal job search sites are listed here (in the order of perceived usefulness by the author) to help you in your job search:

- http://www.monster.com
- http://www.paralegal-job.com
- http://www.paralegaljobs.org
- http://www.paralegaljobs.com
- http://www.lawjobs.com
- http://www.indeed.com
- http://www.ihirelegal.com
- http://www.craigslist.com
- http://www.lawinfo.com
- http://www.careerbuilder.com
- http://www.hotjobs.com

Government positions are generally listed for each individual city, county, or state. However, federal government paralegal positions available across the country and abroad are listed at several sites, including

- http://www.usajobs.opm.gov (official job site of the federal government)
- http://www.fedworld.com (U.S. Department of Commerce)

- http://www.ajb.dni.us (America's Job Bank)
- http://www.govspot.com
- http://www.publicservice.monster.com
- http://www.governmentjobs.com

Although these are not exhaustive lists of all employment databases, they include some of the most useful sites for applicants to paralegal positions.

E-mail Notification

Find a searchable database that provides e-mail notification when a new job posting in your field and your geographical location comes up. You do not want to have to log onto every employment site each day for current listings. Let the sites do the work for you; they want to find qualified job applicants for the employers who pay for their services.

Resume Builders

Most job sites allow you to upload your resume directly to their database. However, many of them also offer resume builders that provide step-by-step guidance to help you build an on-line resume. The builders allow you to choose a format from design templates. You then fill in the sections or respond to the prompts and the builder inserts your information into the template, building your resume in front of you. Once you have your resume, you can print it out or cut and paste it into other job search sites. If you are having trouble getting started, this a great option for you.

Some sites, such as USA Jobs, the official federal government job listing site, provide a simple resume builder free of charge. This site can be found at http://www.usajobs.opm.gov. Other sites, such as http://www.resumebuilder.com, offer the same service, with a few more bells and whistles, for a nominal fee. Take a moment to look at some of these resume builders. You might find a resume format that works for you.

⊙ GO: Start Surfing

No job search is complete without at least a cursory review of on-line paralegal job listings. Even if you do not find a position in your area, consider what other job markets have to offer in terms of opportunity, salary, and benefits. You may find relocating to be an attractive alternative now or in the future. So surf away and something on the Web just might catch your attention.

⊙ Points to Consider

1. *Create an Electronic Resume.* Convert your resume into a plain text resume, following these guidelines:
   - omit formatting
   - use left margin alignment
   - omit bolding, italicization, underlining

- omit shadow boxes
- use all capitals to emphasize material
- replace bullets with + or > or *
- replace lines with =
- use one font style
- do not use tab, line, or paragraph indents

2. ***Create a Fax Resume.*** Print a resume for fax submissions on the basis of the following guidelines:
   - print your resume on a laser printer
   - use white 8½ × 11-inch paper
   - use standard paper weight
   - avoid underlining and shadowing
   - list your name at the top of each page

● Job Search Tips

1. ***Research On-line Databases.*** Visit the following job search databases, along with others listed above, for an overview of paralegal positions available in your area:
   - http://www.monster.com
   - http://www.paralegal-job.com
   - http://www.paralegaljobs.org
   - http://www.paralegaljobs.com
   - http://www.lawjobs.com
   - http://www.indeed.com

2. ***Posting Your Resume.*** Some job seekers find posting their resume on databases such as http://www.monster.com to be effective, and many have found paralegal positions this way. Review the possibilities for each site to determine whether this is an option you would like to consider.

CHAPTER 10

PREPARING FOR THE INTERVIEW
The Final Stage

The interview is your final sales pitch; let the employer know that you are professional, dependable, and prepared.

INTERVIEW PREPARATION

- RESEARCH THE FIRM
- DRESS PROFESSIONALLY
- BRING INTERVIEW ESSENTIALS
- BE PROMPT

Winning an interview is exciting. Your cover letter and resume have opened the door for you to meet personally with the employer. At this stage, you can be confident of the following: you have met the employer's minimum qualifications for the job and something in your resume or cover letter has sparked the employer's interest so he or she now wants to see how you will "fit in" with the office crowd. This is your chance to make a positive impression, so it is crucial that you prepare properly for the interview.

① READY: **Research the Law Firm**

Once you have been offered an interview, you should research the firm and its attorneys to prepare for the interview. The most effective sources for information on a law firm and its attorneys are

- the Internet
- Martindale-Hubbell
- the legal community

Internet Search

Many law firms maintain their own Web site to advertise their services or provide information about their practice areas and attorneys. Therefore, the simplest way to learn about a firm that has extended an interview is to run an Internet search on the firm. This will help you to learn about the location(s) of the firm, its size, and its practice focus, as well as providing short biographies about its attorneys. Print out information about the firm so you can refer to it before the interview. Do not overlook information about the attorneys if it is provided. Attorneys are always impressed when you know where they went to law school or are familiar with some of the clients they have represented.

OFFICE MANAGER

"WHEN A CANDIDATE COMES TO AN INTERVIEW WITH SOME BACKGROUND ABOUT OUR FIRM, IT TELLS ME THAT SHE IS THOROUGH IN HER PREPARATION. SHE HAS OBVIOUSLY DONE SOME RESEARCH BEFORE THE INTERVIEW, PARTICULARLY IF SHE KNOWS SOMETHING ABOUT THE INDIVIDUAL ATTORNEYS—THAT REALLY BLOWS OUR SOCKS OFF. THIS TYPE OF PREPARATION TELLS US THAT THIS APPLICANT WILL LIKELY GO THE EXTRA MILE WHEN SHE IS PREPARING OUR DOCUMENTS AND DOING OUR LEGAL RESEARCH."

Martindale-Hubbell

Many law firms are listed with Martindale-Hubbell, commonly known as "the attorney yellow pages." Martindale-Hubbell is available in most law libraries, or on the Internet at http://www.martindale.com, and provides valuable information about those firms that pay for a listing. You can gain points with a simple statement that indicates your research: "So I understand your primary practice focus is employment law, representing employers." Using this resource will benefit you greatly in your job search.

Legal Community

The legal community can provide an applicant important information about a firm and its culture. Contact attorneys and other paralegals in your community and ask them whether they are familiar with the firm. This is a great way to find out whether the firm is a place you would want to work.

Your instructors may also be helpful in your attempt to learn about firms in the community. Ask your instructors whether they are familiar with a particular firm; you may be surprised to find out that the firm has gone through several paralegals in a very short time. This usually indicates that the firm is not an employee-friendly environment and may not be an ideal employment opportunity.

⦿ SET: Create a Professional Image

Preparing for the interview requires more than researching the firm and its attorneys. You must create a professional image. Dress professionally, bring appropriate interview materials, and plan ahead. From your first contact with the firm, the employer will be asking, "Will this person represent our firm in a professional manner?"

Dress Professionally

As a general rule, law firms are conservative and expect their employees to reflect this image in their appearance and attitudes. This does not mean that all law firms are stuffy and boring, but when a client is paying $350 an hour for an attorney, he wants to feel he is getting a reliable and professional individual. The same goes for office personnel—which means you. The interview is a chance for an employer to evaluate your level of professionalism. This is judged in large part on the basis of your personal appearance and dress.

So, practically speaking, what does it mean to dress appropriately? For most law firms, wear a suit, preferably blue or black; business casual is not considered appropriate for an interview. If you do not own a suit, buy, beg, or borrow one. In addition, men should wear a tie, and women should wear low-key jewelry (e.g., no big gold loop earrings). Neither women nor men should wear perfume or aftershave; surprisingly, perfume overkill is a major complaint of interviewers.

DOES YOUR PERSONAL APPEARANCE PORTRAY A PROFESSIONAL IMAGE? EMPLOYERS WANT TO HIRE EMPLOYEES WHO WILL APPROPRIATELY REPRESENT THEIR FIRM.

You may know attorneys who dress poorly, who do not comb their hair, and who do not shave. Well, here is the difference: they are attorneys and they have jobs. You are looking for a job. So wear a suit, comb your hair, shave, and put on some deodorant. If you are an individual who refuses to put on professional attire and you will not change your purple hair color, then you may find that there are a limited number of employers who are willing to hire you, and you might just have to wait until the right employer comes along. These are choices that have to be made.

Attention Smokers

Do not smoke before an interview. Non-smokers can generally detect the smell, even at a distance. Many offices are non-smoking and may not want to hire a smoker, for a variety of reasons. The firm's insurance rates may increase, smokers are viewed by some employers as less productive because of their need for frequent breaks, smokers statistically have higher rates of absenteeism for health reasons, other staff members may be particularly sensitive to the smell, and, for some employers, it is simply a personal bias.

What to Bring

There are a few essentials that every interviewing paralegal should bring to an interview:

- three copies of your resume
- a list of references
- a pen and legal pad
- a portfolio
- a silent cell phone

Your Resume

Take three copies of your resume to the job interview. Although you have already sent a copy of your resume to the firm (that is how you got the interview), more than one person may interview you at the firm. You should have a resume for each person. It is awkward for two interviewers to have to share your resume. Also, you may meet separately with additional interviewers, and you want to make sure that they have a copy of your professional resume.

Reference List

Prepare your list of references in advance of the interview. Provide a full name, position/title, company name, address, telephone number, and e-mail address for each reference. Use teachers, previous employers, supervisors, professors, and others with whom you have worked for references. Do not use family members or friends who have not worked with you. This is not professional, and their recommendation will not be viewed as reliable.

ATTORNEY

"IF WE HAVE A PARTICULARLY GOOD CANDIDATE IN OUR OFFICE FOR AN INTERVIEW, WE LIKE TO HAVE HER MEET WITH SEVERAL OF OUR PARTNERS TO MAKE SURE THAT EVERYONE WILL BE COMFORTABLE WITH HER. THIS MEANS THAT A CANDIDATE MAY INTERVIEW WITH THREE OR FOUR PEOPLE DURING THE INITIAL INTERVIEW. A GOOD CANDIDATE WILL KNOW THAT IS A POSSIBILITY AND COME TO THE INTERVIEW PREPARED."

If you use a current employer for a reference, do so only with the expectation that the interviewer will call the employer. If you do not want your employer to know that you are looking for a new job, do not list him or her as a reference.

It is best to make a written request to use an individual as a reference. It is common for teachers, in particular, to be unable to place the name and face when a prospective employer calls about a student. It helps to give the reference a brief background of his or her interactions with you (e.g., "I was in your Business Law class in 2005 and received an A on all assignments and exams."). You can hope your reference will be familiar enough with you that you do not need to provide a "remember me" section; however, it is not uncommon for references to receive calls and wonder, "The name is familiar but . . . "

If you have not checked with your references before you list them, you may be asking for trouble. When a reference hesitates about providing a recommendation, a prospective employer may assume that the hesitation is because the employee did not make a positive impression. This certainly does not bode well for an applicant, so do your homework by making contact with your references before a prospective employer does.

Many applicants are under the mistaken impression that a past or present employer cannot legally make any negative statements about an employee. Although there are limitations on discussing sensitive personnel issues or alleged misconduct, an employer can discuss objectively verifiable issues (e.g., "She was always late for work."). However, even a simple hesitation in response to a question such as "Why are they no longer with your firm?" will likely suggest that an applicant would not make a desirable employee. So choose your references wisely.

It is generally expected that a candidate will offer three references. A reference listing should be on a separate sheet of paper and should have your name and contact information at the top of the page (follow the format of your resume). A typical listing should contain name, position/title, company name, address, telephone number, and e-mail address:

Nancy J. Wisehard
Executive Assistant to the President
Northeast CableVision
5678 Main Street
City, State 81150
(999) 555-1212
nwisehard@northeast.com

Employers do call references, so be sure that the contact information is current. As a final note, make sure that your name is listed on the top of the page in case your reference listing is separated from your resume.

Pen and Legal Pad

It is always a good idea to have a pen and legal pad with you so that you do not have to ask to borrow a pen or paper. You want to be as prepared as possible. You may be asked to call a particular person to schedule a follow-up interview, so be prepared to write down his or her name and contact information. In addition, it is good to write down the name of each person who interviewed you. This will allow you to refer to these individuals in a follow-up conversation or send a thank-you note after the interview.

Portfolio

Employers often ask for a writing sample during the interview. A writing sample is the best indication of the type of work you will produce for a law office. Therefore, it is best to have a portfolio of your work prepared for the interview just in case you are asked.

> **HIRING MANAGER**
>
> "APPLICANTS WHO COME TO AN INTERVIEW WITH A PORTFOLIO OF THEIR WRITING SAMPLES IMPRESS ME. IT GIVES ME A GOOD IDEA OF THE QUALITY OF DOCUMENTS THAT THEY WILL PREPARE FOR OUR FIRM."

You can use documents that you have prepared for courses or documents you have created for previous employers. If you use coursework, make sure to use corrected versions. Do not give an employer the version with the instructor's red marks; make the changes suggested by your instructor. If you offer documents prepared for a client, make sure that you provide either a copy of a publicly filed document or a copy with confidential client information omitted. This is a clear sign of professionalism, or lack thereof.

Although a complete portfolio is not necessary for an interview, it is helpful for an employer to review samples of your work product. A portfolio can be a simple file folder that has documents that you have prepared tabbed and indexed. Documents that are typically included in a portfolio are client correspondence, interoffice memoranda, pleadings (complaint, summons, answer, reply, cross-claim, counterclaim), discovery documents (interrogatories, requests for admissions or production), and motions. If you are using actual client documents, you must omit any confidential client information; this point cannot be overstated. Portfolios are generally important for employers when they are interviewing recent graduates without extensive legal experience; they want to see what types of documents the candidate has prepared and to review the quality of work that he or she is able to produce. This can be an invaluable resource for an employer making the decision of which candidate to hire.

Silent Cell Phone

It is good to have a cell phone with you on your way to an interview. If you are running late, you can call the employer and let them know—of course, they may not want to interview you if you are not prompt. However, leave the phone in the car or turn it off; you do not need it during an interview. Inevitably a cell phone will go off during an interview. This interrupts the flow of the interview, whether or not the call is answered. Do not just set your phone on vibrate; turn it off.

If, in your anxiety to get to the interview, you forget to turn off your cell phone and it rings during your meeting, *do not answer it.* This

HIRING MANAGER

"I HAD AN APPLICANT WHO WAS ON A PERSONAL CALL WHEN SHE WALKED INTO MY OFFICE FOR HER FIRST IN-TERVIEW. SHE HELD UP HER FINGER TO TELL ME THAT SHE WOULD JUST BE A MIN-UTE. HER RESUME DID NOT PARTICULARLY IMPRESS ME IN THE FIRST PLACE, SO I TOLD HER THAT I DIDN'T HAVE A MINUTE AND HAD MY SECRETARY ESCORT HER OUT."

is incredibly unprofessional and indicates that you do not value the employer's time. An employee who prioritizes personal calls during an interview is also one who will prioritize personal calls over work that needs to be performed for the firm. Clearly, this does not make a good impression.

▶ GO: Start Interviewing

Preparing for the interview can be as important as the interview itself. Take the time to research the firm and its attorneys. Make sure that you dress professionally and take the necessary items to the interview. And last, but by no means least, be prompt. A candidate who presents him or herself professionally at an interview will be more likely to land the job.

◉ Points to Consider

1. *Prepare a Professional Portfolio.* Prepare a portfolio of documents for writing samples to provide at an interview. A portfolio can include documents prepared for coursework or client documents that you have prepared. If you provide current client documents, you must omit any identifying information that may be deemed confidential. Documents that can be included in a portfolio are
   - client correspondence
   - interoffice memoranda
   - pleadings (complaint, summons, answer, reply, cross-claim, counterclaim)
   - discovery documents (interrogatories, requests for ad-missions or production)
   - motions
2. *Compile Interview Essentials.* Assemble documents and items that you will need for an interview. Preparing these in advance will prevent a last-minute rush or, worse, for-getting these items for an interview. Necessary interview items include
   - three copies of your resume
   - a list of references
   - a pen and legal pad
   - a portfolio
   - a silent cell phone

◉ Job Search Tips

1. *Research Martindale-Hubbell.* Conduct an Internet search through http://www.martindale.com on a firm of interest to you.
2. *Research Firm Web sites.* Before an interview, read through the firm's Web site materials.

CHAPTER 11

THE INTERVIEW
The Final Stage

The interview is a two-way street. Be prepared to ask questions to determine whether you want to work for the firm with which you are interviewing.

**KEYS TO A
SUCCESSFUL
INTERVIEW**

- BE PROMPT
- BE PREPARED
- BE POSITIVE

The interview begins as soon as you walk into the office, so do not underestimate the importance of your first impression on the office staff. Some applicants view the interview with great anticipation; others view this stage with trepidation. The interview should be viewed as an opportunity to promote yourself and to learn about the law office and the people who work there. Remember, you need to determine whether this is a place where you want to work. If you happen to have a bad interview, do not worry about it; consider it an practice interview and learn from the experience.

Before you begin your interviewing process, it may be helpful to contact law firms in your area for an "informational interview." This is an opportunity to meet with a paralegal or attorney and ask them questions about the legal profession. Informational interviews are great because they allow you the opportunity to meet with legal professionals in a more relaxed environment—without the stress of a job on the line—and to learn how to interact with the legal community. Consider making these initial contacts as an investment in your future. You never know, an informational interview may even turn into a job opportunity because the firm is so impressed with your professionalism.

ⓘ READY: The First Impression Is Lasting

You arrive for an interview as soon as you step into the office building. This applies whether the law firm owns the whole building or there are several offices within a complex. You need to be nice to the people in the hallway, in the elevator, and in the restrooms; you never know who works for the firm. If someone accidentally lets the entry door slam on you and you are rude, you may just have shut the door on your interview—what if the person at the door was your interviewer? So be courteous to everyone.

When you arrive at the law office, tell the receptionist who you are and that you have an interview with Mr. or Ms. Blank regarding the paralegal position. Do not smoke, chew gum, or eat while waiting for the interviewer. Make sure that you are pleasant with everyone in the office; if you are not, the hiring manager will hear about it.

When you meet the interviewer, stand up and shake hands. Tell him or her that you appreciate the opportunity to meet to discuss the position. If the interview is conducted in the interviewer's office, it is helpful to break the ice by mentioning something about the décor of the office, such as school or sports memorabilia or family pictures. In general, the interviewer will try to put you at ease and start asking questions; however, it never hurts to have a back-up plan to connect with your interviewer.

Be Prompt

The best way to make a good first impression is to be prompt; prompt means be ten minutes early. Plan appropriately, even if this means you have to wait in the coffee shop next door for an hour. Being late makes one of the worst impressions. You will forever be referred to as "that paralegal who was late for her interview."

Be Prepared: Job Applications

Occasionally, employers ask people applying for paralegal or legal assistant positions to complete a job application when they arrive for an interview. Although this is not the norm for private law firms, government positions almost always require that you complete an application. It is wise to check all hiring criteria to determine whether an application is part of the hiring process so that you can arrive at the interview prepared. The forms are often available on-line.

Job applications are very straightforward and ask for much of the same information that is on your resume. However, applications generally ask for additional information, including, but not limited to, the following.

- *Names of previous supervisors.* Applications generally ask you to list the names of your previous supervisors. This allows the firm to contact a person who has direct experience of you as an employee.
- *Address and telephone number for previous employers.* Applications often ask you to provide addresses and phone numbers of previous employers. You may need to have this information with you if you cannot recall it from memory.
- *Job history.* Your job history on an application is broadly similar to the history listed on your resume. However, applications often ask for specific dates of employment, including months, which may not be available on your resume. You may also be required to list employment that is not on your resume if you have omitted job listings from your resume because of space limitations.

- *Criminal history.* Job applications often ask whether you have ever been convicted of a felony. You must answer honestly, as employers will often run a background check to determine this.
- *Education.* Applications frequently ask for specifics about your educational background, including the name and address of the high school that you attended.

Although job applications are usually not required for paralegal positions, be prepared with the appropriate information in case you are asked to complete one.

Be Positive

During the interview, be positive about your previous job experiences, your previous employers, and your job responsibilities. Interviewers do not like to hear stories about how awful your last job was or what a horrible supervisor you had. Negative stories suggest that you were dissatisfied with the work and that you may be the one with whom it is difficult to work. This does not sit well with prospective employers.

⑪ SET: Be Set to Answer Zinger Questions

What happens when the employer asks you those zinger questions to which there is no right answer? "Tell me about your weaknesses." It can be difficult to answer such questions if they are thrown at you, but with a little coaching and practice, you can learn how to respond appropriately.

What Is Legal and What Is Not

Although most employers are careful to avoid discriminatory lines of questioning, interviewers can and do cross the line of what is legal and what is not. Do not assume that just because you are interviewing with a law firm, the interviewer will avoid inappropriate questions. Issues that an employer may not raise during the selection process include

- age
- race
- nationality
- religion
- marital status
- family/children
- unrelated criminal history
- sexual orientation
- disabilities

If you are asked a question about any of these issues, you are not required to answer and you should report the questioning to the managing partner—assuming the managing partner is not the person interviewing you. You do not want to work for an unethical office, so do not feel pressured into providing an answer.

PARALEGAL

"GO WITH YOUR GUT
FEELING. IF THERE IS
SOMETHING ABOUT THE
INTERVIEW OR THE PERSON
INTERVIEWING YOU THAT
MAKES YOU UNCOMFORT-
ABLE, THE JOB IS PROBABLY
NOT ONE THAT YOU WANT.
REMEMBER, YOU HAVE TO
SPEND EIGHT HOURS A DAY,
FIVE DAYS A WEEK AT YOUR
JOB. THAT'S A LOT OF TIME.
YOU NEED TO BE HAPPY
OR IT WILL FEEL LIKE
ETERNITY."

However, rather than giving a tirade on your rights under Title VII of the Civil Rights Act, consider the purpose in the employer's line of questioning. If an employer asks about your family life, he or she may really be trying to get at whether your personal commitments will interfere with your work schedule. Be prepared to answer such questions with a generic response: "I have always been able to successfully balance my personal commitments with my professional obligations." This response addresses their concerns and also lets them know you are aware that the question was inappropriate.

⏵ GO: Facing the Interviewer

Interviewers love to see how applicants will respond to hard-to-answer questions that are open-ended. Be prepared to answer these questions with concise and direct responses. Below are a few of the favorite zingers of interviewers, with commentary.

- *Tell me about yourself.*

This is a great opportunity to tell the employer about your professional experience and how you are qualified for this position. If you do not have a clear direction, such open-ended questions can lead to rambling. Limit your answer to no more than two or three minutes. It is best to avoid mentioning that a messy divorce or a run-in with the law led to your interest in pursuing a legal career.

- *Tell me about your background.*

You will always be asked to describe your background, including your work history. Some interviewers want a general idea of who you are, such as where you grew up and how long you have lived in the area. Remember, however, that you should not respond to this question with an in-depth discussion of personal information. You do not need to discuss your marital or family situation.

- *What is your relevant experience?*

Be prepared to discuss your relevant work experience. Summarize your legal experience, including job responsibilities, such as word processing, document preparation, client interviewing, and legal research (mention your proficiency with on-line research databases such as Lexis-Nexis or WESTLAW).

Although the employer is targeting legal experience, if you do not have a legal background, discuss the skills you developed in your paralegal educational program, such as document preparation, interviewing, and legal research skills. Also consider how job positions you have held outside of the legal profession will benefit you in your paralegal career. Mention any relevant experience from previous jobs: word processing, management, financial background checks, customer service, bookkeeping, and so on. Do not short-change yourself here; you have more relevant experience than you think.

- *What are your strengths and weaknesses?*

In answering this question, focus on your strengths and qualifications for the job. Do not provide the employer with a laundry list of your weaknesses! The stock answer for this question is "I'm a perfectionist" or "I'm a workaholic and get overly involved in my work." Turn your "weakness" into a positive for the employer.

• *What do you find appealing about this particular position?*
Although you may find nothing unique about the position you are currently interviewing for, you need to think of a professional response. Do not say, "I just really need a job and I am not particular about where I work. I'm just trying to get my foot in the door." Mention information about the firm: "I like the idea of working in a larger/smaller firm. It will offer me a wider range of experiences" (this response works in both large and small firms); "I want to work with an estate planning/construction defect/family law firm." Get the picture? Just pick something about the firm and mention how you would like to work in that environment.

• *What are your life goals?*
Describe your personal goals. The answer can be generic: "I'm seeking personal and professional fulfillment." Do not talk about how you want to make a ton of money and retire as early as possible. If you are involved in community service, mention this and how you hope to make a difference in the world: "I volunteer with the Special Olympics and I hope that I can make a difference in a family's life."

• *What are your professional goals?*
In responding to this question, you need to consider how your goals will match the firm's goals for their employees. You may note that you hope to become an asset to a legal practice through your hard work and skills. It sounds good to mention that you would like to be an integral part of an attorney's practice and feel that it is important to develop a professional relationship that allows your attorney to hand you any project and know that it will be completed professionally and in a timely manner.

• *How well do you work with others?*
Ok, you know this response: "I have always been able to work cooperatively with others in any work setting." This is not the time to tell the employer that in your last job everyone was so difficult to get along with that you finally decided you had to leave. If you have had a string of jobs and have consistently found colleagues uncooperative or hostile, it may be time to look at your own behavior. Most people are not hard to get along with; therefore, look at yourself honestly and consider whether you are the one who is difficult.

• *Tell me about your worst employment experience.*
Watch out with this one. The employer is trying to determine whether you are a "blamer." Are you going to assign the responsibility for a bad employment experience to your boss, or are you willing to take some responsibility for a negative situation? Hopefully, you have not had such employment experiences, but if you have, be careful here. Do not point the finger at a previous employer, and certainly do not tell a potential employer that you had an obnoxious boss. Take responsibility, if necessary, and indicate that "I learned a lot from the experience, particularly how to respond flexibly to the needs and demands of others."

• *Are there obstacles to working extra hours, as needed?*

If you are a workaholic, this may be a good time to point out that you are generally available to stay until your responsibilities are complete. However, many people are not able to work additional hours on a regular basis. Therefore, a good defense is sometimes a direct question: "How often do your employees generally work after hours?"

Be honest about whether this works for you. You can let the employer know that you are occasionally available for additional work. However, if this just will not work with your schedule, you need to say, "I'm a team player and will try to be available when you need me. I do have personal commitments that require that I maintain regular hours." This sets the expectation, and either it works for the firm or it does not, but you have been direct. This is helpful later if an employer consistently asks you to work extra hours. You can remind them that you stated in your interview that your personal commitments require you to maintain designated hours.

• *What do you know about this position?*

This is a goldmine if you have done your research before the interview. Firms like to know that you are willing to take the extra step and will research all available information. Remember to check Martindale-Hubbell (http://www.martindale.com) and firm Web sites, or just do a Google search of the firm or the attorney as you prepare for the interview. Make a copy of this information and take it with you to review while you are waiting for the interviewer. Attorneys are impressed when you know about their firm or, better yet, when you know something about them. If you have done research and could not find anything on the firm, it is worth noting that you checked Martindale-Hubbell and the Web but could not find information about the firm. At least they know that you are a researcher.

• *Are you looking for career advancement?*

So, are you? Most attorneys are Type-A personalities and respect someone who is looking to advance his or her career. However, if you are being interviewed by another paralegal, you need to be careful about your response. You should not say, "I want to be the lead paralegal in the firm," if that position is currently held by the interviewing paralegal. A response such as "Yes, I would like to maximize every opportunity" lets the employer know that you are motivated but does not challenge anyone personally. You may also want to consider responding with "What opportunities for advancement does the firm offer?"

• *What style of employee are you?*

Here, the employer is trying to determine whether you can work independently or whether you will need significant direction with projects. Employers want to be comfortable handing you a project and knowing that you will get it done. At the same time, they need to know that you will feel comfortable asking questions when you need direction. A good response is "I am an independent worker, but I know when to ask questions."

• *Why do you want to be a paralegal?* or *Why are you changing jobs?*

When you are changing career paths or looking for a new job in the same career, you need to be prepared to explain to an employer why you are shifting gears. Employers like to hear "I'm looking for a new challenge in my work." This suggests that you are motivated to learn and continue to grow professionally.

- *What are your hobbies?*

Employers are looking for well-rounded employees. The current thinking is that happy people make good employees who are productive and get along well with others. So tell the employer about your activities and outside interests.

- *I notice that you have little or no paid job experience.*

This is an issue often raised with homemakers who have recently entered the job market. In answering this question, focus on the skills you developed as a volunteer and the opportunities that your experiences presented to you.

The employer may be attempting to elicit information about your family. If your children are grown, tell the employer that you raised three wonderful children and had the opportunity to be home with them during their impressionable years. However, now you are a seeking a career that allows you to contribute to your community.

If you have young children, do not tell the employer how hard it is to keep a paid job when you are driving them to their doctors' appointments, caring for them when they are sick, or finding time to volunteer in their school. Focus on the positive aspects of your community involvement as a volunteer.

- *How many children do you have?*

This question is a human resource nightmare. Employers are not allowed to ask about your family life, but many do anyway, so be prepared to address the issue tactfully. An appropriate response would be "I have always been able to balance my personal life with my professional life." Some employers may be offended that you have not directly answered their question, but this will also put them on notice that you are aware that the question is improper and will prevent similar follow-up questions from being asked.

- *Are you aware of anything that would limit your ability to perform the tasks of this job position?*

This is the politically correct way for an employer to ask the question "I notice that you have some disabilities; will this require any accommodation on our part?" An interviewer should not specifically refer to the limitations of a prospective employee and will likely ask for this information indirectly. However this question is posed, be prepared to answer it honestly. If you have limitations that require accommodation, tell the employer what your needs are, particularly if your disability is obvious during the interview. Employers will appreciate an open and honest approach, and it will put them at ease to know what will be expected of them in the event they hire you.

- *Where do you see yourself in ten years?*

This is a "What do you want to be when you grow up?" question. Focus on where you want to be professionally: "In ten years I hope to be an indispensable asset as a paralegal to a law firm's practice."

● *What are your salary requirements?*

Employers often want to know what your salary expectations are regarding the job. Rather than mentioning a specific figure and undervaluing or overvaluing yourself, it is best to say "The going rate for this type of work is . . ." and offer a broad salary range. Be prepared to tell the employer the source of your information, such as a recent survey conducted by a paralegal association or state bar association or other relevant material.

Some employers will ask directly, "What is it you need to make in a new position?" You should be familiar with the salaries being paid for paralegals with your experience in the area. Therefore, you can simply state that you are expecting to earn between *X* and *Y*. Some employers want you to be specific about your salary requirements, so be prepared to answer this question directly if called upon to do so.

● *May I contact your current employer for a reference?*

Most prospective employers want a reference from a current or past employer, and the answer to this question varies according to your circumstances. If your current employer is aware that you are looking for a new job and you know that he or she will provide a positive reference, tell the interviewer that it is fine to contact your employer. However, if your current employer has no idea that you are looking for a new job, you want to be prepared to let an interviewer know you would prefer that they not make contact; you also want to avoid stumbling over your answer and making it seem as if you are hiding something. A good response is simply "I have a very positive relationship with my current employer and I do not want to jeopardize my employment status. I am looking for a new opportunity that will allow me to expand my career path."

● *Do you have any questions?*

You should view the interview as an opportunity to ask questions and learn about the job and the firm. Most interviewees allow the employer to ask all of the questions without determining whether they would like the job if it is offered to them. However, this is also an opportunity to let the employer know that you have prepared for the interview and have certain expectations. Some appropriate questions are

– how many paralegals do you have?
– what are the primary responsibilities of the paralegals in the firm?
– do the firm's paralegals work primarily with one attorney or with several?
– what created this job opening? Why is this job available?
– what is your vision for this position? What responsibilities come with the job?
– what type of documents do your paralegals produce? (pleadings, discovery, motions)
– what do I need to do to be successful in this position?
– what is the average work week for a paralegal in the firm? (This is a professional way of asking how many hours you will be expected to work).

– what is the turnover rate for paralegals in this firm?

– what opportunities for advancement are available?

Make sure that you find out enough about the job position to make an informed decision in the event you receive an offer.

Follow-Up: Thank-You Note

It is important to write a follow-up letter to thank the interviewer for taking the time to meet with you. Handwritten notes are often recommended, to add a personal touch, but many employers prefer to see a thank-you letter that is typed as an additional example of your writing ability and professionalism. Write down the name of each person with whom you have a conversation. Better yet, ask each interviewer for a business card at the conclusion of the interview. Compose a letter on your computer and send it off *immediately* after the interview. This will remind the employer of your interest in the job and associate your name with the position. A typical thank-you note might read as follows:

January 3, 2008

Kim Harth, Esq.
Harth & Gamble
23 Main Street
Nowhere, State 98079

Dear Ms. Harth,

Thank you for meeting with me yesterday to discuss the paralegal position available with your firm. I enjoyed our conversation and learning about your firm's practice.

I am very interested in joining Harth & Gamble as a paralegal and having the opportunity to work with the attorneys in your firm. I look forward to hearing from you regarding the position.

Sincerely,

Megan Bryant
789 South Avenue West
Missoula, Montana 89052
(406) 555-9087

Do not forget to write your thank-you note; it is the firm's last impression of your interview.

A Final Word

Working as a paralegal will offer you a challenging and rewarding professional career. As you search for your ideal job opportunity, remember that you want to find a position that you will enjoy and that will meet your needs, personally and professionally. You have worked hard to become a paralegal, and you should now reap the rewards of your endeavor.

◉ Points to Consider

1. *Practice Responding to Zingers.* Ask a friend or family member to fire zinger questions at you to help you prepare your responses to tough questions that may be asked during a job interview.

2. *Prepare Your Questions.* Prepare a written list of questions you would like to ask about the firm with which you will be interviewing. Use these questions to help you determine whether you want to work for this employer.

◉ Job Search Tips

1. *Illegal Interview Questions.* Use the Internet to research specific questions that cannot be asked of a candidate during the interview process. Enter the search term "illegal interview questions" and review the information provided. Consider how you might answer these questions if they are asked of you.

2. *Get Directions.* Avoid delays by getting directions to a law firm well in advance of your scheduled interview. You can contact the firm and ask for directions or obtain them through http://www.mapquest.com.

CHAPTER 12

CLOSING THE DEAL
The Offer Phase

If you need to negotiate the terms of an offer, carefully consider how to approach this. It is not always what you say, but how you say it, that matters.

ESTABLISHING JOB CRITERIA

- WORK ENVIRONMENT
- JOB RESPONSIBILITIES
- CLIENT CONTACT
- WORK HOURS
- BILLABLE HOUR REQUIREMENTS
- POTENTIAL FOR ADVANCEMENT
- SALARY OFFER
- BENEFITS PACKAGE (HEALTH CARE, RETIREMENT, ETC.)
- CONTINUING EDUCATION
- PERSONAL ECONOMICS (PERSONAL EXPENSES, DAY CARE COSTS, ETC.)
- LOCATION
- TRANSPORTATION TIME
- TRANSPORTATION COSTS
- EMPLOYMENT STABILITY

When a job offer comes your way, you have to be prepared to close the deal. Before you even receive an offer, however, you should consider the criteria for determining whether a job opportunity is right for you. Thinking about this beforehand will help you to respond appropriately to an offer, whether you accept it right away or ask for time to consider your options.

① READY: Evaluating a Job Offer

You must evaluate any job offer on the basis of your personal and professional priorities, as well as the practicality of the offer package as a whole. If this is your first job in the paralegal field or you are in a tight job market, you may not have the luxury of waiting for a job that meets all of your criteria. Enough cannot be said about the value of "sweat equity." However, there are basic economic factors that must be considered for any employment situation. If you cannot pay for your food, clothing, housing, transportation, day care, and other necessities on this salary, you may need to consider other options. Create a list of your priorities to help you evaluate whether potential job offers will be a good fit with your needs.

Establishing Job Criteria

Although each person's job criteria will vary, several factors should always be considered in determining whether a job meets your personal and professional criteria. These include

- work environment
- job responsibilities
- client contact
- work hours

117

- billable hour requirements
- potential for advancement
- salary offer
- benefits package (health care, retirement, etc.)
- continuing education
- personal economics (personal expenses, day care costs, etc.)
- location
- transportation time
- transportation costs
- employment stability

Some of these items obviously carry more weight than others. Creating a list of your own priorities will help you to evaluate your expectations better when a job offer comes your way.

⑪ SET: Accepting or Rejecting an Offer

Many job seekers mistakenly think that they have to accept a job offer immediately. Employers understand that applicants often need time to consider an offer, particularly if the compensation package was not discussed during the interview. A simple "That sounds great. Why don't I give you a call Friday" indicates that you are definitely interested but you need time to think it over.

Although most offers are extended verbally, employers often send an offer confirmation letter containing the specifics of salary and benefits. Employers will let you know if an offer letter is coming; tell them that you will get back to them as soon as you receive it.

Employers understand that you may need a day or two to consider an offer. However, it is unlikely that they will wait for more than a few days; if they do not hear back from you, they will simply move down their list of candidates. Some employers will not even give you a follow-up call if they have not heard from you; they will assume that you do not want the job because you have not called. Do not risk this. Be specific about when you will get back to them, and call the firm back even if you are not accepting their offer. This is basic professional courtesy. You never know when you may be applying to their firm again, so leave them with a positive impression.

When to Negotiate

If a job offer falls short of your expectations, you may consider negotiating the compensation package. However, if an employer perceives you to be too demanding, the offer may be withdrawn. This is a balance that only you can weigh to determine whether negotiating is worth the risk.

In determining whether you can return to the offer table, think back to comments made by the employer during the interview. Is the offer at the bottom of the salary range that the employer suggested the firm would be paying? If you sensed that there was flexibility in the terms of the offer, consider opening this discussion.

PARALEGAL

"AFTER I EARNED MY PARALEGAL CERTIFICATE, I RECEIVED A GREAT OFFER FROM A FIRM ACROSS TOWN. HOWEVER, WHEN I STARTED FIGURING OUT THE ADDITIONAL DAY CARE EXPENSES I WOULD HAVE BECAUSE OF THE TWO-HOUR ROUND-TRIP COMMUTE, AS WELL AS MY TRAVEL COSTS, I REALIZED THAT I COULDN'T AFFORD TO TAKE THE JOB. I ACCEPTED A JOB CLOSER TO MY HOME. EVEN THOUGH THE JOB PAID SLIGHTLY LESS, I WAS ACTUALLY MAKING MORE WHEN I FACTORED IN THE ADDITIONAL COSTS I WOULD HAVE INCURRED WITH THE JOB ACROSS TOWN."

If the salary is significantly lower than the range for paralegals in your area, it is appropriate to make a statement such as "The salary offer is below the market rate. Is the compensation package flexible?" Other appropriate responses might include:

- I will be making less than I am in my current position. Is the compensation package negotiable?
- What are the opportunities for performance bonuses?
- Is it possible to re-evaluate the salary to correlate with my current earnings?

If the employer is not able or willing to re-evaluate the compensation, consider other options that might be available if you want this particular job. Questions that could be raised are:

- Would the employer be willing to increase your compensation package on the basis of your quarterly performance?
- Is a hiring bonus an option?
- Can you negotiate additional vacation or sick leave?
- Would the employer be willing to consider allowing you to work fewer hours?

These are simply options that you may want to consider if the salary is significantly lower than you expected. However, be careful not to seem too demanding in your requests, or you may find that you no longer have an offer to consider. On the other hand, you do not want to be miserable with your new job because you did not negotiate the terms to fit your needs. This is a balancing act that only you can perform.

⑪ ALMOST SET: Leaving Your Employer

Once you decide to accept a new offer and it is time to notify your current employer, make sure that you leave on good terms. Employers generally know when their employees have been looking for other positions and are not necessarily surprised when they are informed that you will be moving on. However, it is important to maintain professional relationships; you never know when you will need to call upon a previous employer for a reference or a professional favor.

You should give your employer at least two weeks' notice to find a replacement. If you have more time, offer to train the new paralegal and bring him or her up to speed. It is not uncommon for a departing paralegal to be asked to find his or her replacement. If this task is assigned to you, be enthusiastic with the new hire. Do not criticize your employer or share gossip about other staff members. This type of behavior will invariably come back to bite you. Remain positive and offer constructive guidance to the new paralegal about the office and internal procedures.

Before you leave your employer, prepare a status memo on current assignments that you are not able to complete. Do not expect that verbal statements to the new paralegal about the status of pending matters will be remembered. Type a short memo and leave it in the file for each case that was assigned to you.

⊙ GO: Opportunity Awaits: Starting Your New Job

As you begin your new job, make sure to start out on the right foot. Be enthusiastic, be early for work, be willing to skip breaks, and be open to taking on new tasks. Maintain your professional standards and do not hesitate to ask questions. Clarify job duties, assignments, and expectations. If you are given a particular task, ask when it should be completed. You have a new opportunity for professional growth, and you should take full advantage of it.

The duties of a paralegal are not set in stone. Most law firms are willing to give a paralegal any project that he or she demonstrates an ability to handle. View each assignment as an opportunity to demonstrate your value to the firm. If you do so, you will undoubtedly gain great personal satisfaction working as a paralegal. May you have great success in your job search and in your paralegal career.

⊙ Points to Consider

1. *Establish Your Personal Job Criteria.* Consider the criteria for your ideal job position and create a personalized listing. This will help you objectively evaluate job offers that you receive.
2. *Prepare Discussion Issues for Salary Negotiations.* Before receiving a job offer, you must establish your minimum acceptable salary requirements. In the event that you receive an offer below this amount but are otherwise interested in the job, prepare a list of comments for discussion that will allow you to negotiate a salary increase with the employer.

⊙ Job Search Tips

1. *Research Salary Surveys.* During your job search, research salary and compensation packages generally offered in your area. This information can be obtained from your local bar or paralegal association.
2. *Professional Overview.* The U.S. Department of Labor, Bureau of Labor Statistics, *Occupational Outlook Handbook, 2006–2007 Edition,* "Paralegals and Legal Assistants" (http://www.bls.gov/oco/ocos114.htm) provides a national overview of job placement, salary, and demographics for paralegals.

CHAPTER 13

A FINAL NOTE

Ethical Considerations for Freelance Paralegals

Paralegals may work as independent contractors for attorneys. However, paralegals should not plan on hanging their own shingles and providing services directly to the public. This road usually leads to trouble.

PARALEGAL ETHICS: RULES AND GUIDELINES

- STATE STATUTES
- LEGAL OPINIONS
- NFPA MODEL CODE OF ETHICS AND PROFESSIONAL RESPONSIBILITY
- NALA CODE OF ETHICS AND PROFESSIONAL RESPONSIBILITY
- NATIONAL, STATE, AND LOCAL PARALEGAL ASSOCIATION RULES
- ABA MODEL GUIDELINES FOR THE UTILIZATION OF LEGAL ASSISTANT SERVICES

Some paralegals dream of opening their own office and being their own boss; however, be aware that there are two ways to accomplish this end: one road leads to opportunity, the other can lead you to trouble. If being your own boss is your goal, be aware of the fork in the road. Going into business for yourself with the intent of providing freelance paralegal services to attorneys may allow you some control over your work schedule. Paralegals can perform a variety of freelance services for attorneys, including, but not limited to, case management, legal research, witness and client interviews, factual investigation, and document preparation. However, the second path, hanging your own shingle and providing services directly to the public, is likely to lead to trouble. Paralegals are generally restricted by state statute and/or court opinions from providing legal services directly to the public without the supervision of an attorney.

In 1991, the American Bar Association (ABA) adopted the ABA Model Guidelines for the Utilization of Legal Assistant Services (Model Guidelines) to provide attorneys with "useful and authoritative guidance in working with paralegals."[i] In accordance with the ABA's Model Rules of Professional Conduct (Model Rules), attorneys must directly supervise a paralegal to ensure that the paralegal's conduct is consistent with the attorney's ethical and professional obligations. The ABA's Model Guideline 1 provides

[a] lawyer is responsible for all of the professional actions of a paralegal performing services at the lawyer's direction and should take reasonable measures to ensure that the paralegal's conduct is consistent with the lawyer's obligation under the rules of professional conduct of the jurisdiction in which the lawyer practices.

The ABA's Model Rules, applicable to attorneys, recognize that attorneys are professionally responsible for the conduct of their paralegals.

The ABA Model Guidelines are "addressed to lawyer conduct and not directly to the conduct of the paralegal";[ii] however in addition, most states have specific statutory provisions prohibiting the "unauthorized practice of law." Such statutes serve as the basis for legal actions against paralegals who provide services to the public without attorney supervision. Furthermore, national, state, and local paralegal associations impose corresponding limitations on their members.

Legal Document Preparers

Over the past several years, many states have seen a rise in the number of paralegals who provide legal services directly to the public. Most states prohibit these actions, and all state bar associations actively oppose such services being provided by paralegals. Some states, including Arizona, Washington, and Florida, have created a category of "independent paralegals," known most commonly as "legal document preparers," who are allowed to provide basic document preparation services to the public without the supervision of an attorney. California also allows a corresponding category of legal professionals, known as "legal document assistants"; however, these professionals are prohibited from using the title "paralegal."

States that allow legal document preparers strictly regulate their activities and generally prohibit this category of legal professionals from providing legal advice to clients, including, but not limited to, selecting forms for clients or advising clients about the legal ramifications of particular forms. In other words, legal document preparers are allowed to prepare forms chosen by their clients, but they cannot give legal advice to clients about the forms themselves. Furthermore, the forms that are used by legal document preparers must be drafted or otherwise approved by a licensed attorney. These regulatory provisions are intended to protect the public from the unauthorized practice of law.

① READY: Professional Paralegal Association Guidelines

The paralegal profession is not yet governed by a uniform code of conduct; instead, the profession is generally regulated by state statutory provisions or court opinions addressing paralegal ethics. In addition, national, state, and local professional paralegal associations promulgate guidelines for their members. Although these ethical codes are not uniformly binding on the paralegal profession, they offer a framework of appropriate professional standards.

Notably, the National Association of Legal Assistants (NALA) and the National Federation of Paralegal Associations (NFPA), two of the prominent national paralegal associations, have adopted ethical codes for their respective organizations to "delineate the principles for ethics and conduct to which every paralegal should aspire."[iii] These codes of conduct are instructive with regard to all aspects of the paralegal profession and specifically restrict paralegals from performing legal work directly for the public.

NALA's Code of Ethics and Professional Responsibility, Canon 3, provides, in relevant part:

A legal assistant must not: (a) engage in, encourage, or contribute to any act which could constitute the unauthorized practice of law; and (b) establish attorney-client relationships, set fees, give legal opinions or advice or represent a client before a court or agency unless so authorized by that court or agency.

Similarly, the NFPA's Model Code of Ethics and Professional Responsibility and Guidelines for Enforcement provide that "[a] paralegal shall comply with the applicable legal authority governing the unauthorized practice of law in the jurisdiction in which the paralegal practices."[iv] Each of these paralegal associations specifically restricts paralegals from providing legal advice directly to the public without the "shield" of attorney supervision.

⑪ SET: Understanding the Rationale

You may believe that some legal services that attorneys perform require no more than filling out a standardized form—something that you could easily do. So, why is it that paralegals cannot prepare these forms for anyone who is willing to pay? First, completing seemingly "simple" forms requires legal judgment, and this constitutes the practice of law. Second, it is simply not allowed. A paralegal who openly advertises his or her services is not likely to fly under the radar of the respective enforcement authority forever.

So why are all of these regulations imposed on paralegals? State bar associations carefully regulate the practice of law in each state to establish and maintain professional standards in the legal profession, thereby protecting the public from untrained legal professionals. To put it simply, consider that attorneys have spent years studying the law, thousands of dollars paying for their legal education, and months enduring the agony of the bar exam. Attorneys would soon be out of work if paralegals could perform the same services for a fraction of the price. Of course, attorneys have additional training and expertise in the law, which allows them to offer a comprehensive analysis of the legal situation. Moreover, what seems like a simple "fill-in-the-blanks" exercise actually requires some level of legal judgment.

For example, consider Articles of Incorporation, the initial document that legally "creates" a corporation. This form seems pretty simple, but it is not. Even before choosing the corporate form, a client needs to be informed about the different organizational options available to a business. Then the client needs to consider which organizational form best suits the needs of his or her business. Would a limited liability partnership, a corporation, or a limited liability company be the best form for this type of business (or would some other form be better)? Next the client needs information about establishing the capital structure of the company. How will the company be financed? If a corporation seems to meet the requirements of the client's business, the client needs legal guidance on the number of shares that should be issued, the value of each share, and whether to issue preferred stock. Most paralegals are not aware of the complexity of the legal factors that must be considered *before* an attorney chooses to file a seemingly simple document such as Articles of Incorporation. The same rationale applies to the thousands of other "simple" forms that may be completed by a paralegal under the direction of a supervising attorney.

Some states recognize the complexities of choosing and completing forms for clients and specifically prohibit paralegals from such actions. For example, in Nevada a paralegal is prohibited from choosing which legal document a client should complete, and violations of the statutory limitations on the practice of law are treated as a felony offense.[v] Other states have followed suit, and the state bar associations in every state campaign to limit the role of paralegals in providing services directly to the public. Many paralegals fly under the radar of the regulating authority by titling their services as "document preparation services," as discussed above. However, each state has specific limitations on such practices, and you should review the applicable provisions for your own area.

In accordance with state regulation of the legal profession, virtually every paralegal program instructs its students not to venture into the workplace with the intent to provide services directly to the public. Obviously, this road has many potholes along the way.

Liability Considerations

Just in case you missed the sign in the road and you are still considering opening your own office and working with anyone who is willing to pay your fees, consider the potential liability that paralegals face in providing legal services to the public. Although I am sure you believe that you would never make a mistake or professional misjudgment, mistakes can and do happen. Many legal professionals learn this far too late and bankrupt themselves trying to defend legal actions brought against them, whether or not they are justified.

Whereas most practicing attorneys have malpractice insurance to protect them in the event of a claim, a paralegal who is not working in compliance with state law cannot obtain this "first line of defense." As a result, if a claim is brought against a paralegal who has provided legal services directly to the public, the paralegal will have to finance his or her own legal defense, which can cost thousands, if not tens of thousands, of dollars. In addition, any monetary award to a prevailing client would come out of the paralegal's own pocket. To add salt to the wound, the paralegal's misconduct would likely come to the attention of the state prosecutor's office, and civil or criminal charges might be brought against the paralegal. So now how do you feel about filling out one of those "simple" forms?

Neighbor Law

The most common area of law for any attorney or paralegal is what some refer to as "neighbor law." You may never have heard of this area of law—but you will. It crops up every day as your neighbors, friends, and family ask you for free legal advice. Many people you know will innocently ask you a simple legal question, and some may ask you whether you can prepare legal documents for them. It is tempting to do so, particularly for a close family member, but be careful.

Although many paralegals believe that they would never violate professional canons of ethics and offer their services directly to the public, they inadvertently do just that when they prepare the paperwork for a cousin's divorce, compile incorporation documents for a friend's new business, or prepare a complaint for "a little matter" on behalf of their brother. Of course, all of your friends and family promise, "Oh, I'll never tell anyone that you helped me." Your good intentions will, at some point, be rewarded; however, they may not be a rewarded in the way that you would like. All too often, a family member will freely tell the judge or the opponent's attorney, "Well, my sister-in-law is a paralegal and prepared all of the paperwork for me; I guess she didn't know what she was doing." Then there you are, exposed to the legal world for your philanthropic indiscretion. It is likely that you will be the next defendant in that judge's courtroom. It cannot be stressed enough how your good intentions will create landmines on the road to your professional success.

Many instructors would tell you that a paralegal is not giving legal advice if he or she provides only general information. However, problems arise when the information provided is incorrect or the listener/client hears something totally different from what was said and relies upon it. This is when you hear a client say, "But my paralegal told me . . . "—to the court and others. Obviously, this can and does lead to problems. Therefore, it is helpful to have a prepared response for all of those who surround you with legal questions and want some quick advice. Tell them that there are many legal issues to be considered and you can give them the name of a great attorney whom you would seek out if you were in the same situation.

If you do not know the name of a great attorney who specializes in a particular area of law, call any attorney whom you respect and have a connection with; he or she will generally be able to direct you to someone in another practice area. So be prepared to respond to your family and friends with a referral to an attorney who can appropriately and professionally handle their matter.

▶ GO: Freelance Paralegal Services

Clearly, there are ethical limitations on paralegals hanging their own shingle and providing legal services directly to the public. However, paralegals can and do open their own offices to provide freelance services to attorneys. Through freelance work, paralegals commonly perform the same services that in-house paralegals provide to attorneys. For example, a freelance paralegal can prepare legal documents, conduct client interviews, prepare the attorney for trial, conduct factual investigations, and carry out legal research. Under the supervision of an attorney, all of these services can be offered by paralegals to the legal community.

Preparing to Fly Solo

Although you may have a burning desire to be your own boss and work on a freelance basis for attorneys in the community, many paralegals choose to begin their careers with an established attorney or law firm to gain experience in the legal profession. This practical experience proves useful in terms of learning the practices and procedures of law firms and the courts before launching an independent service. By tapping into these available resources, you can increase your marketability when you later open an independent office to provide paralegal services for the legal community.

If you use your first job as a training ground for a later venture, be observant of the policies, procedures, and office workings as a whole. Tap into the resources and become familiar with the intake procedures for legal documents; calendaring of projects and deadlines; computer programs used for client billing, office expenses, and payroll; and the legal research materials used by the firm. Learning how to create, manage, and maintain a law practice effectively and efficiently will benefit you when you launch your own office.

In addition, use your position in an established firm to begin networking in the legal community, whether inside the firm you are working for or with paralegals, attorneys, or staff in other firms. Create a name for yourself through your quality of work and professionalism. Many paralegals who leave their law firm often return to work on a contract basis for the firm or are asked to do freelance work for other offices they previously worked with (often including the opponent's office). The key is to establish that you are reliable and professional in your communications and your work product. Never overlook the incredible opportunities that are available with the proper background and connections.

Independent Contract Services

If you decide to offer your paralegal services to the legal community, make sure that you establish guidelines and standards and incorporate them into a written contract that you can present to an attorney *before* you begin work. A contract should include a brief description of the assignment, the project due date, the rate of pay, and the paralegal's access to the firm's resources (copy machines, Lexis-Nexis/WESTLAW accounts, law library, and so on). By the time you develop an ongoing relationship with an attorney, you will undoubtedly have established all of these points; however, until that time, a written contract will help to prevent misunderstandings.

In determining your billing rate, consider whether you will charge an hourly rate or a stated per project fee. Most law firms prefer an hourly charge, which they pass along to their client. However, keep in mind that a firm expects to add their overhead costs (office space, law library, copy costs, and so on) to your charges. Therefore, they will add one-third to one-half to the rate you charge the firm. Bear this in mind when establishing your fees and make sure they align with those of other freelance services. Obviously, a firm will not consider hiring you if your charges, coupled with their overhead costs, are significantly higher than the going rate for paralegal services.

If you are unsure what your charges should be, call other services and ask what they charge. Many services will freely provide this information to you, and a law firm itself might tell you what they generally pay for freelance services. Make sure you do your research before you offer your services to attorneys and law firms.

Although working your own hours as a freelance paralegal may seem like a desirable choice, it works best for those who are very self-disciplined. Some people find it difficult to maintain their workload if they do not have regularly scheduled work hours. In addition, many freelance services are home-based, which means that your work hours become blurred with your personal time. In deciding whether to choose the traditional route of working for an attorney or freelancing your paralegal services to the legal community, talk to other paralegals about the opportunities that are available in your area, as well as the pros and cons of working for yourself.

As a final note, as you explore your employment options, strive to maintain a balance between your personal and professional life. Too many paralegals and attorneys sacrifice themselves for their careers. Determine your priorities in life. Do you want to work to live or live to work? The choice is yours.

◉ Points to Consider

1. *Review Ethical Codes.* Review the ethical codes of the National Association of Legal Assistants and the National Federation of Paralegal Associations, both available in the Appendix, as well as the ethical provisions of your state or local paralegal associations. Consider the specific limitations imposed on paralegals offering their services to the public.
2. *Research State Statutes.* Research your state's statutory provisions restricting the unauthorized practice of law.
3. *Research Relevant Case Law.* Research case law from your jurisdiction addressing the appropriate duties of paralegals. If no case law is available from your state or local courts, review opinions from other jurisdictions that have considered the limitations on paralegals providing legal services directly to the public.

◉ Job Search Tips

1. *Contact Freelance Paralegals.* Contact freelance paralegals in your area who are providing services to the legal community. If you cannot find a listing of these individuals, ask attorneys or other legal professionals for referrals.
2. *Research Contract Terms.* Research freelance paralegal contract provisions and prepare a sample contract on the basis of your review. Consider provisions for project as-

signments, project due dates, rate of pay, and access to the firm's resources, including copy machines, Lexis-Nexis/ WESTLAW accounts, and the firm's law library.

3. ***Contact Attorneys and Law Firms.*** Begin making a list of attorneys and law firms that use the independent contract services of paralegals.

◉ References

[i] Preamble, ABA Model Guidelines for the Utilization of Paralegal Services (2003) (http://www.abanet.org).

[ii] Id.

[iii] Preamble, NFPA Model Code of Ethics and Professional Responsibility and Guidelines for Enforcement (http://www.paralegals .org). See also the appendix to this book.

[iv] NFPA EC-1.8(a).

[v] See David A. Clark, Status Report: Unauthorized Practice of Law Initiative, 9 *Nevada Lawyer* 30, March 2001; Nev. Rev. Stat. section 7.285 (2001).

ETHICAL GUIDELINES FOR PARALEGALS

National Federation of Paralegal Associations, Inc., Model Code of Ethics and Professional Responsibility

Reprinted by permission of the National Federation of Paralegal Associations, Inc., http://www.paralegals.org.

NFPA Model Disciplinary Rules and Ethical Considerations

Section 1.1. A PARALEGAL SHALL ACHIEVE AND MAINTAIN A HIGH LEVEL OF COMPETENCE.

(a) A paralegal shall achieve competency through education, training, and work experience.

(b) A paralegal shall aspire to participate in a minimum of twelve (12) hours of continuing legal education, to include at least one (1) hour of ethics education, every two (2) years in order to remain current on developments in the law.

(c) A paralegal shall perform all assignments promptly and efficiently.

Section 1.2. A PARALEGAL SHALL MAINTAIN A HIGH LEVEL OF PERSONAL AND PROFESSIONAL INTEGRITY.

(a) A paralegal shall not engage in any ex parte communications involving the courts or any other adjudicatory body in an attempt to exert undue influence or to obtain advantage or the benefit of only one party.

(b) A paralegal shall not communicate, or cause another to communicate, with a party the paralegal knows to be represented by a lawyer in a pending matter without the prior consent of the lawyer representing such other party.

(c) A paralegal shall ensure that all timekeeping and billing records prepared by the paralegal are thorough, accurate, honest, and complete.

(d) A paralegal shall not knowingly engage in fraudulent billing practices. Such practices may include, but are not limited to: inflation of hours billed to a client or employer; misrepresentation of the nature of tasks performed; and/or submission of fraudulent expense and disbursement documentation.

(e) A paralegal shall be scrupulous, thorough and honest in the identification and maintenance of all funds, securities, and other assets of a client and shall provide accurate accounting as appropriate.

(f) A paralegal shall advise the proper authority of non-confidential knowledge of any dishonest or fraudulent acts by any person pertaining to the handling of the funds, securities or other assets of a client. The authority to whom the report is made shall depend on the nature and circumstances of the possible misconduct, (e.g., ethics committees of law firms, corporations and/or paralegal associations, local or state bar associations, local prosecutors, administrative agencies, etc.). Failure to report such knowledge is in itself misconduct and shall be treated as such under these rules.

Section 1.3. A PARALEGAL SHALL MAINTAIN A HIGH STANDARD OF PROFESSIONAL CONDUCT.

(a) A paralegal shall refrain from engaging in any conduct that offends the dignity and decorum of proceedings before a court or other adjudicatory body and shall be respectful of all rules and procedures.

(b) A paralegal shall avoid impropriety and the appearance of impropriety and shall not engage in any conduct that would adversely affect his/her fitness to practice. Such conduct may include, but is not limited to: violence, dishonesty, interference with the administration of justice, and/or abuse of a professional position or public office.

(c) Should a paralegal's fitness to practice be compromised by physical or mental illness, causing that paralegal to commit an act that is in direct violation of the Model Code/Model Rules and/or the rules and/or laws governing the jurisdiction in which the paralegal practices, that paralegal may be protected from sanction upon review of the nature and circumstances of that illness.

(d) A paralegal shall advise the proper authority of non-confidential knowledge of any action of another legal professional that clearly demonstrates fraud, deceit, dishonesty, or misrepresentation. The authority to whom the report is made shall depend on the nature and circumstances of the possible misconduct, (e.g., ethics committees of law firms, corporations and/or paralegal associations, local or state bar associations, local prosecutors, administrative agencies, etc.). Failure to report such knowledge is in itself misconduct and shall be treated as such under these rules.

(e) A paralegal shall not knowingly assist any individual with the commission of an act that is in direct violation of the Model Code/Model Rules and/or the rules and/or laws governing the jurisdiction in which the paralegal practices.

(f) If a paralegal possesses knowledge of future criminal activity, that knowledge must be reported to the appropriate authority immediately.

Section 1.4. A PARALEGAL SHALL SERVE THE PUBLIC INTEREST BY CONTRIBUTING TO THE IMPROVEMENT OF THE LEGAL SYSTEM AND DELIVERY OF QUALITY LEGAL SERVICES, INCLUDING PRO BONO PUBLICO SERVICES.

(a) A paralegal shall be sensitive to the legal needs of the public and shall promote the development and implementation of programs that address those needs.

(b) A paralegal shall support efforts to improve the legal system and access thereto and shall assist in making changes.

(c) A paralegal shall support and participate in the delivery of Pro Bono Publico services directed toward implementing and improving access to justice, the law, the legal system or the paralegal and legal professions.

(d) A paralegal should aspire annually to contribute twenty-four (24) hours of Pro Bono Publico services under the supervision of an attorney or as authorized by administrative, statutory or court authority to:

1. persons of limited means; or
2. charitable, religious, civic, community, governmental and educational organizations in matters that are designed primarily to address the legal needs of persons with limited means; or
3. individuals, groups or organizations seeking to secure or protect civil rights, civil liberties or public rights.

The twenty-four (24) hours of Pro Bono Publico services contributed annually by a paralegal may consist of such services as detailed in this EC-1.4(d), and/or administrative matters designed to develop and implement the attainment of this aspiration as detailed above in EC-1.4(a) B (c), or any combination of the two.

Section 1.5. A PARALEGAL SHALL PRESERVE ALL CONFIDENTIAL INFORMATION PROVIDED BY THE CLIENT OR ACQUIRED FROM OTHER SOURCES BEFORE, DURING, AND AFTER THE COURSE OF THE PROFESSIONAL RELATIONSHIP.

(a) A paralegal shall be aware of and abide by all legal authority governing confidential information in the jurisdiction in which the paralegal practices.

(b) A paralegal shall not use confidential information to the disadvantage of the client.

(c) A paralegal shall not use confidential information to the advantage of the paralegal or of a third person.

(d) A paralegal may reveal confidential information only after full disclosure and with the client's written consent; or, when required by law or court order; or, when necessary to prevent the client from committing an act that could result in death or serious bodily harm.

(e) A paralegal shall keep those individuals responsible for the legal representation of a client fully informed of any confidential information the paralegal may have pertaining to that client.

(f) A paralegal shall not engage in any indiscreet communications concerning clients.

Section 1.6. A PARALEGAL SHALL AVOID CONFLICTS OF INTEREST AND SHALL DISCLOSE ANY POSSIBLE CONFLICT TO THE EMPLOYER OR CLIENT, AS WELL AS TO THE PROSPECTIVE EMPLOYERS OR CLIENTS.

(a) A paralegal shall act within the bounds of the law, solely for the benefit of the client, and shall be free of compromising influences and loyalties. Neither the paralegal's personal or business interest, nor those of other clients or third persons, should compromise the paralegal's professional judgment and loyalty to the client.

(b) A paralegal shall avoid conflicts of interest that may arise from previous assignments, whether for a present or past employer or client.

(c) A paralegal shall avoid conflicts of interest that may arise from family relationships and from personal and business interests.

(d) In order to be able to determine whether an actual or potential conflict of interest exists a paralegal shall create and maintain an effective recordkeeping system that identifies clients, matters, and parties with which the paralegal has worked.

(e) A paralegal shall reveal sufficient non-confidential information about a client or former client to reasonably ascertain if an actual or potential conflict of interest exists.

(f) A paralegal shall not participate in or conduct work on any matter where a conflict of interest has been identified.

(g) In matters where a conflict of interest has been identified and the client consents to continued representation, a paralegal shall comply fully with the implementation and maintenance of an Ethical Wall.

Section 1.7. A PARALEGAL'S TITLE SHALL BE FULLY DISCLOSED.

(a) A paralegal's title shall clearly indicate the individual's status and shall be disclosed in all business and professional communications to avoid misunderstandings and misconceptions about the paralegal's role and responsibilities.

(b) A paralegal's title shall be included if the paralegal's name appears on business cards, letterhead, brochures, directories, and advertisements.

(c) A paralegal shall not use letterhead, business cards or other promotional materials to create a fraudulent impression of his/her status or ability to practice in the jurisdiction in which the paralegal practices.

(d) A paralegal shall not practice under color of any record, diploma, or certificate that has been illegally or fraudulently obtained or issued or which is misrepresentative in any way.

(e) A paralegal shall not participate in the creation, issuance, or dissemination of fraudulent records, diplomas, or certificates.

Section 1.8. A PARALEGAL SHALL NOT ENGAGE IN THE UNAUTHORIZED PRACTICE OF LAW.

A paralegal shall comply with the applicable legal authority governing the unauthorized practice of law in the jurisdiction in which the paralegal practices.

National Association of Legal Assistants, Code of Ethics

Copyright 2007, adopted 1975; revised 1979, 1988, 1995. Reprinted with permission of the National Association of Legal Assistants, http://www.nala.org, 1516 S. Boston #200, Tulsa, Oklahoma 74119.

Canon 1.

A legal assistant must not perform any of the duties that attorneys only may perform nor take any actions that attorneys may not take.

Canon 2.

A legal assistant may perform any task which is properly delegated and supervised by an attorney, as long as the attorney is ultimately responsible to the client, maintains a direct relationship with the client, and assumes professional responsibility for the work product.

Canon 3.

A legal assistant must not: (a) engage in, encourage, or contribute to any act which could constitute the unauthorized practice of law; and (b) establish attorney-client relationships, set fees, give legal opinions or advice or represent a client before a court or agency unless so authorized by that court or agency; and (c) engage in conduct or take any action which would assist or involve the attorney in a violation of professional ethics or give the appearance of professional impropriety.

Canon 4.

A legal assistant must use discretion and professional judgment commensurate with knowledge and experience but must not render independent legal judgment in place of an attorney. The services of an attorney are essential in the public interest whenever such legal judgment is required.

Canon 5.

A legal assistant must disclose his or her status as a legal assistant at the outset of any professional relationship with a client, attorney, a court or administrative agency or personnel thereof, or a member of the general public. A legal assistant must act prudently in determining the extent to which a client may be assisted without the presence of an attorney.

Canon 6.

A legal assistant must strive to maintain integrity and a high degree of competency through education and training with respect to professional responsibility, local rules and practice, and through continuing education in substantive areas of law to better assist the legal profession in fulfilling its duty to provide legal service.

Canon 7.

A legal assistant must protect the confidences of a client and must not violate any rule or statute now in effect or hereafter enacted controlling the doctrine of privileged communications between a client and an attorney.

Canon 8.

A legal assistant must do all other things incidental, necessary, or expedient for the attainment of the ethics and responsibilities as defined by statute or rule of court.

Canon 9.

A legal assistant's conduct is guided by bar associations' codes of professional responsibility and rules of professional conduct.

INDEX

Note: *Italic* page numbers indicate material in tables or figures.

PERSONAL INFORMATION

Name _____

Address _____

City_____ State_____ Zip_____

If at this address less than 2 years:

Previous Address _____

City_____ State_____ Zip_____

Phone number   (h) (_____) _____-_____

                (w) (_____) _____-_____

Date of birth   ____/____/____
                 mo   day year

Place of birth City_____ State_____

U.S. citizen   Yes_____ No_____

Social Security number _____-_____-_____

Visa number_____ Visa type_____

PROFESSIONAL EXPERIENCE

Employer 1

Name _____

Address _____

City_____ State_____ Zip_____

Job title _____

Reported to _____

Dates of employment   From ____/____/____ To ____/____/____
                            mo   day   year   mo   day   year

Reason for leaving position

_____

_____

Recommendation available   Yes_____ No_____

1. Contact name _____

   Contact title _____

2. Contact name _____

   Contact title _____

Duties and responsibilities

1._____

_____

2._____

_____

3._____

_____

4._____

_____

5. _____

_____

Technology used (software, telecommunication systems)

_____

_____

_____

_____

_____

Equipment used (tools, machinery, hardware)

_____

_____

_____

_____

_____

Accomplishments (qualify in terms of concrete employer-related benefits)

1._____

_____

2._____

_____

3._____

_____

4._____

_____

5. _____

_____

PROFESSIONAL EXPERIENCE

Employer 2

Name _____

Address _____

City_____ State_____ Zip_____

Job title _____

Reported to _____

Dates of employment   From ____/____/____ To ____/____/____
                                mo   day   year   mo   day   year

Reason for leaving position

_____

_____

Recommendation available   Yes_____ No_____

1. Contact name _____

   Contact title _____

2. Contact name _____

   Contact title _____

Duties and responsibilities

1._____

_____

2._____

_____

3._____

_____

4._____

_____

5._____

_____

Technology used (software, telecommunication systems)

_____

_____

_____

_____

_____

Equipment used (tools, machinery, hardware)

_____

_____

_____

_____

_____

Accomplishments (qualify in terms of concrete employer-related benefits)

1. _____

_____

2. _____

_____

3. _____

_____

4. _____

_____

5. _____

_____

PROFESSIONAL EXPERIENCE

Employer 3

Name _____

Address_____

City_____ State_____ Zip_____

Job title _____

Reported to _____

Dates of employment   From ____/____/____ To ____/____/____
                                    mo   day   year   mo   day   year

Reason for leaving position

_____

_____

Recommendation available   Yes_____ No_____

1. Contact name _____

   Contact title _____

2. Contact name _____

   Contact title _____

Duties and responsibilities

1._____

_____

2._____

_____

3._____

_____

4._____

_____

5._____

_____

Technology used (software, telecommunication systems)

_____

_____

_____

_____

_____

Equipment used (tools, machinery, hardware)

_____

_____

_____

_____

_____

Accomplishments (qualify in terms of concrete employer-related benefits)

1. _____

_____

2. _____

_____

3. _____

_____

4. _____

_____

5. _____

_____

PROFESSIONAL EXPERIENCE

Employer 4

Name _____

Address_____

City_____ State_____ Zip_____

Job title _____

Reported to _____

Dates of employment   From ____/____/____ To ____/____/____
                              mo   day year   mo   day year

Reason for leaving position

_____

_____

Recommendation available   Yes_____ No_____

1. Contact name _____

   Contact title _____

2. Contact name _____

   Contact title _____

Duties and responsibilities

1._____

_____

2._____

_____

3._____

_____

4._____

_____

5. _____

_____

Technology used (software, telecommunication systems)

_____

_____

_____

_____

_____

Equipment used (tools, machinery, hardware)

_____

_____

_____

_____

_____

Accomplishments (qualify in terms of concrete employer-related benefits)

1. _____

_____

2. _____

_____

3. _____

_____

4. _____

_____

5. _____

_____

INTERNSHIP EXPERIENCE

Name _____

Address _____

City_____ State_____ Zip_____

Job title _____

Reported to _____

Dates of employment   From ____/____/____ To ____/____/____
                              mo   day   year   mo   day   year

Reason for leaving position

_____

_____

Recommendation available   Yes_____ No_____

1. Contact name _____

   Contact title _____

2. Contact name _____

   Contact title _____

Duties and responsibilities

1. _____

   _____

2. _____

   _____

3. _____

   _____

4. _____

   _____

5. _____

   _____

Technology used (software, telecommunication systems)

_____

_____

_____

_____

_____

Equipment used (tools, machinery, hardware)

_____

_____

_____

_____

_____

Accomplishments (qualify in terms of concrete employer-related benefits)

1. _____

_____

2. _____

_____

3. _____

_____

4. _____

_____

5. _____

_____

INTERNSHIP EXPERIENCE

Name _____

Address_____

City_____ State_____ Zip_____

Job title _____

Reported to _____

Dates of employment   From ____/____/____ To ____/____/____
                            mo   day   year   mo   day   year

Reason for leaving position

_____

_____

Recommendation available   Yes_____ No_____

1. Contact name _____

   Contact title _____

2. Contact name _____

   Contact title _____

Duties and responsibilities

1._____

_____

2._____

_____

3._____

_____

4._____

_____

5. _____

_____

Technology used (software, telecommunication systems)

_____

_____

_____

_____

_____

Equipment used (tools, machinery, hardware)

_____

_____

_____

_____

_____

Accomplishments (qualify in terms of concrete employer-related benefits)

1. _____

_____

2. _____

_____

3. _____

_____

4. _____

_____

5. _____

_____

VOLUNTEER EXPERIENCE

Association/Organization Name_____

Address_____

City_____ State_____ Zip_____

Job title_____

Reported to _____

Dates of employment   From ____/____/____ To ____/____/____
                              mo   day year   mo   day year

Reason for leaving position

_____

_____

Recommendation available   Yes_____ No_____

1. Contact name _____

   Contact title _____

2. Contact name _____

   Contact title _____

Duties and responsibilities

1._____

_____

2._____

_____

3._____

_____

4._____

_____

5._____

_____

Technology used (software, telecommunication systems)

_____

_____

_____

_____

_____

Equipment used (tools, machinery, hardware)

_____

_____

_____

_____

_____

Accomplishments (qualify in terms of concrete employer-related benefits)

1. _____

_____

2. _____

_____

3. _____

_____

4. _____

_____

5. _____

_____

VOLUNTEER EXPERIENCE

Association/Organization Name_____

Address_____

City_____ State_____ Zip_____

Job title_____

Reported to _____

Dates of employment   From ____/____/____ To ____/____/____
                              mo day year   mo day year

Reason for leaving position

_____

_____

Recommendation available   Yes_____ No_____

1. Contact name _____

   Contact title _____

2. Contact name _____

   Contact title _____

Duties and responsibilities

1._____

_____

2._____

_____

3._____

_____

4._____

_____

5. _____

_____

Technology used (software, telecommunication systems)

_____

_____

_____

_____

_____

Equipment used (tools, machinery, hardware)

_____

_____

_____

_____

_____

Accomplishments (qualify in terms of concrete employer-related benefits)

1._____

_____

2._____

_____

3._____

_____

4._____

_____

5. _____

_____

MILITARY EXPERIENCE

Branch of Service _____

Service Number _____

Armed Forces Code _____

Service Number _____

Honorable discharge   Yes___ No___

Registered with Selective Service   Yes___ No___

Vietnam Era veteran   Yes___ No___

Disable veteran   Yes___ No___

Reason for leaving military

_____

_____

Recommendation available   Yes_____ No_____

1. Contact name _____

    Contact title _____

2. Contact name _____

    Contact title _____

Duties and responsibilities

1. _____

    _____

2. _____

    _____

3. _____

    _____

4. _____

    _____

5. _____

    _____

Technology used (software, telecommunication systems)

_____

_____

_____

_____

_____

Equipment used (tools, machinery, hardware)

_____

_____

_____

_____

_____

Accomplishments (qualify in terms of concrete employer-related benefits)

1._____

_____

2._____

_____

3._____

_____

4._____

_____

5._____

_____

Program	Institution	From		To	
		mo.	yr.	mo.	yr.
High School	Name: _____ _____ Address: _____ _____ City_____ State_____ Zip_____				
College	Name: _____ _____ Address: _____ _____ City_____ State_____ Zip_____				
Other	Name: _____ _____ Address: _____ _____ City_____ State_____ Zip_____				
Other	Name: _____ _____ Address: _____ _____ City_____ State_____ Zip_____				
GED	Date Received ____ / ____ mo. yr.				

VOCATIONAL TRAINING

Area of Study	Credit Hours Completed	Diploma/ Degree Certificate	Date Granted		Grade Point Average
			mo.	yr.	
Major: Minor:					
Major: Minor:					
Major: Minor:					
Major: Minor:					

City _____ State _____

CAREER OBJECTIVES

Job title 1. _____

Job title 2. _____

Preferred salary $_____

Start date ____/____/____
            mo day year

Preferred schedule   Mon.–Fri. _____

                      Other _____

Weekends   Yes____ No____

Holidays   Yes____ No____

Overtime   Yes____ No____

Relocation   Yes____ No____

Preferred locations   1. _____

                      2. _____

                      3. _____

Professional Memberships

Organization name _____

Organization name _____

Professional Certifications/Licenses

Type_____ exp. date_____

Type_____ exp. date_____

Personal interests (hobbies, leisure activities)

1._____

2._____

3._____

4._____

5._____

PERSONAL REFERENCES

Reference 1

Name_____

Address_____

City_____ State_____ Zip_____

Phone (w) _____ phone (h) _____

Relationship _____ Number of years known _____

Received resume or work history? Yes___ No___

Reference 2

Name_____

Address_____

City_____ State_____ Zip_____

Phone (w) _____ phone (h) _____

Relationship _____ Number of years known _____

Received resume or work history? Yes___ No___

Reference 3

Name_____

Address_____

City_____ State_____ Zip_____

Phone (w) _____ phone (h) _____

Relationship _____ Number of years known _____

Received resume or work history? Yes___ No___

PROFESSIONAL REFERENCES

Reference 1

Name _____

Title _____

Company name _____

Address _____

City_____ State_____ Zip_____

Phone _____ ext. _____

Received resume or work history? Yes___ No___

Reference 2

Name _____

Title _____

Company name _____

Address _____

City_____ State_____ Zip_____

Phone _____ ext. _____

Received resume or work history? Yes___ No___

Reference 3

Name _____

Title _____

Company name _____

Address _____

City_____ State_____ Zip_____

Phone _____ ext. _____

Received resume or work history? Yes___ No___

Reference 4

Name _____

Title _____

Company name _____

Address _____

City_____ State_____ Zip_____

Phone _____ ext. _____

Received resume or work history? Yes___ No___

Reference 5

Name _____

Title _____

Company name _____

Address _____

City_____ State_____ Zip_____

Phone _____ ext. _____

Received resume or work history? Yes___ No___

FREQUENTLY ASKED INTERVIEW QUESTIONS

- Why are you interested in working for us?
- Tell me about yourself. What are your strengths?
- What is your major weakness?
- What interests you most about this job?
- Do you work better alone or in a group?
- What do you know about our organization?
- What do you like to do in your spare time?
- How would you describe your personality?
- Which of your accomplishments have given your the greatest satisfaction?
- How would you define your long-range career goals?
- Why are you leaving your present job?
- Do you have any questions for me?

QUESTIONS YOU SHOULD ASK

Asking questions demonstrates your interest in the position.

- What do you like and dislike most about the organization?
- How do you see your organization developing over the next few years?
- What would be the highest priority for me to accomplish if you hired me?
- If you were to offer me the job, where could I expect to be five years from now?

ADDITIONAL QUESTIONS YOU WISH TO ASK

1. _____
_____
_____

2. _____
_____
_____

3. _____
_____
_____

4. _____
_____
_____

5. _____
_____
_____

6. _____
_____
_____

7. _____
_____
_____

8. _____
_____
_____

9. _____
_____
_____

10. _____
_____

WHEN YOU ARE LEAVING THE INTERVIEW

- Offer a firm handshake while expressing your thanks to the interview.
- Mention that you are eagerly looking forward to hearing from them.
- Always be courteous to the secretary or assistant upon leaving the office.

FOLLOW UP AFTER THE INTERVIEW

- Send a thank-you letter.
- Start with a courteous thank you for the interview.
- End with a reiteration of why you want the job and what you can do for the organization.

- One week after the interview, follow up with a phone call.

- If you do not get the job, ask the interviewer for some constructive criticism on your interview technique.

INTERVIEW INFORMATION

Date of interview _____

Company name _____

Company address _____

Interviewer's name _____

Interviewer's title _____

Date of interview _____

Company name _____

Company address _____

Interviewer's name _____

Interviewer's title _____

Date of interview _____

Company name _____

Company address _____

Interviewer's name _____

Interviewer's title _____

Date of interview _____

Company name _____

Company address _____

Interviewer's name _____

Interviewer's title _____

Date of interview _____

Company name _____

Company address _____

Interviewer's name _____

Interviewer's title _____

INTERVIEW INFORMATION

Date of interview _____

Company name _____

Company address _____

Interviewer's name _____

Interviewer's title _____

Date of interview _____

Company name _____

Company address _____

Interviewer's name _____

Interviewer's title _____

Date of interview _____

Company name _____

Company address _____

Interviewer's name _____

Interviewer's title _____

Date of interview _____

Company name _____

Company address _____

Interviewer's name _____

Interviewer's title _____

Date of interview _____

Company name _____

Company address _____

Interviewer's name _____

Interviewer's title _____

INTERVIEW INFORMATION

Date of interview _____

Company name _____

Company address _____

Interviewer's name _____

Interviewer's title _____

Date of interview _____

Company name _____

Company address _____

Interviewer's name _____

Interviewer's title _____

Date of interview _____

Company name _____

Company address _____

Interviewer's name _____

Interviewer's title _____

Date of interview _____

Company name _____

Company address _____

Interviewer's name _____

Interviewer's title _____

Date of interview _____

Company name _____

Company address _____

Interviewer's name _____

Interviewer's title _____

INTERVIEW INFORMATION

Date of interview _____

Company name_____

Company address _____

Interviewer's name_____

Interviewer's title _____

Date of interview _____

Company name_____

Company address _____

Interviewer's name_____

Interviewer's title _____

Date of interview _____

Company name_____

Company address _____

Interviewer's name_____

Interviewer's title _____

Date of interview _____

Company name_____

Company address _____

Interviewer's name_____

Interviewer's title _____

Date of interview _____

Company name_____

Company address _____

Interviewer's name_____

Interviewer's title _____

NOTES